BUILD-IT-YOURSELF
BIRDHOUSES

Inspiring | Educating | Creating | Entertaining

Brimming with creative inspiration, how-to projects, and useful information to enrich your everyday life, Quarto Knows is a favorite destination for those pursuing their interests and passions. Visit our site and dig deeper with our books into your area of interest: Quarto Creates, Quarto Cooks, Quarto Homes, Quarto Lives, Quarto Drives, Quarto Explores, Quarto Gifts, or Quarto Kids.

© 2020 Quarto Publishing Group USA Inc.
Text © 2020 Chris Peterson
Photography © 2020 The Quarto Group

First Published in 2020 by Cool Springs Press, an imprint of The Quarto Group, 100 Cummings Center, Suite 265-D, Beverly, MA 01915, USA. T (978) 282-9590 F (978) 283-2742 QuartoKnows.com

Cool Springs Press titles are also available at discount for retail, wholesale, promotional, and bulk purchase. For details, contact the Special Sales Manager by email at specialsales@quarto.com or by mail at The Quarto Group, Attn: Special Sales Manager, 100 Cummings Center, Suite 265-D, Beverly, MA 01915, USA.

24 23 22 21 20   1 2 3 4 5

ISBN: 978-0-7603-6528-1

Digital edition published in 2019
eISBN: 978-0-7603-6529-8

Library of Congress Cataloging-in-Publication Data

Names: Peterson, Chris, 1961- author.
Title: Build-it-yourself birdhouses : 25+ DIY birdhouses and bird feeders / by Chris Peterson.
Description: Beverly, MA, USA : Cool Springs Press, 2020. | Includes bibliographical references and index. | Summary: "Step-by-step instructions for 25+ unique birdhouses tailored for specific birds-pick the one that fits your neighborhood's birds and get building! Join home improvement pro Chris Peterson as he shares a variety of creative designs for birdhouses and bird feeders, from the classic bluebird house to a mid-century modern home. While all the designs are handsome, most are also approachable for beginning woodworkers. Squares, triangles, and simple joining are used throughout the book. For woodworkers with some experience, Peterson shares a variety of customization techniques that can enhance the designs. Every project contains a showstopping photo of the finished house and step-by-step instructions (with additional photos) to take any guesswork out of the assembly. You'll also find mounting instructions and tips, as well as information on the types of birds each birdhouse can accommodate. Designs include: Small birdhouses: Chickadee Shelter, Nuthatch Wedge, Songbird PVC Birdhouse, Flycatcher Cinderblock Motel, Purple Martin Boarding House, Tufted Titmouse Cabin, Finch's Pub, a Bat Cave, and more! Large birdhouses: Mourning Dove Monster Ledge, American Kestrel Lodge, Barn Owl A-Frame, Barred Owl Nest Box, Wood Duck Slat House, and a Woodpecker's Log House. Creative bird feeders: Telephone Platform Feeder, Porch Swing Bin Feeder, Hanging Man Suet Feeder, Squirrel Proof Feeder, and Zen Feeder"-- Provided by publisher.
Identifiers: LCCN 2019024763 | ISBN 9780760365281 (trade paperback)
Subjects: LCSH: Birdhouses. | Do-it-yourself work.
Classification: LCC QL676.5 .P485 2020 | DDC 598.072/34--dc23
LC record available at https://lccn.loc.gov/2019024763

Cover and Interior Design: tabula rasa graphic design

Printed in China

BUILD-IT-YOURSELF
BIRDHOUSES

25+ DIY Birdhouses and Bird Feeders

CHRIS PETERSON

COOL
SPRINGS
PRESS

CONTENTS

INTRODUCTION

Why build a birdhouse?

It's a fair question. You work hard. You get dinner on the table every night. On weekends, you mow your lawn. You tend your garden. You put effort into making the outside of your house look as nice as the inside. Maybe you put in a flagstone patio. Then, you work some more. You shop for groceries. You do your laundry. And when you can, you want to get outside to relax—no work, just pure enjoyment of the great outdoors.

Birdhouses are a small but visually powerful way to decorate your yard. They allow you to add colorful accents and design touches, from the purely whimsical to the elegantly sophisticated. Building a birdhouse is also a way to have some fun in your garage or shop, creating a project that is not so challenging that it's frustrating, but is most certainly rewarding.

And let's not forget about the real bonus of a birdhouse: inviting beautiful feathered gems to call your yard home over the breeding season (and perhaps beyond). As lovely as any birdhouse can be, the birds that occupy it are beautiful in their own right. They are hypnotizing to watch as they go about their lives gathering food, bathing, and singing. Especially singing. There is no music quite like birdsong, and every bird's song is different. Many species also offer amazing visual displays, splashes of color rarely found in the garden, even among flowers. So, a birdhouse lets you find even more enjoyment in your outdoor spaces.

Of course, yard aesthetics are just the most obvious benefit of building a custom birdhouse. You'll also be helping the environment, by providing a home for birds who have fewer and fewer suitable nesting sites. A German study from 2017 discovered that in the last twenty-five years, the worldwide insect population has diminished by almost 75 percent. Why does that matter? Because the same factors that affect insect life—large scale use of highly toxic pesticides, herbicides, and insecticides and the encroachment of urban and suburban sprawl—are wiping out bird habitats and putting bird populations at the same risk of decline as the insects many of them eat.

All that said, you can choose to simply put up a birdhouse for the appeal it adds to the garden, with no intention of it ever having occupants. However, if you are hoping to attract feathered visitors to the structure, you should realize that birds have very particular requirements for their homes. Like Goldilocks, they prefer something that is not too large and not too small, but with just the right dimensions and the right size entry hole (you'll find all that information, at a glance, in the chart on page 23).

Birds also have preferences for their home's surroundings, regardless of where they actually build a nest. Large expanses of well-tended lawns and tidy networks of roadways won't do. A birdhouse can actually be a really important addition to a bird's world. It can be the rare place where the lovely feathered traveler feels safe and comfortable. It's a sanctuary where birds can not only lodge but, more importantly, reproduce.

Fortunately, meeting birds' needs is not just easy; making a yard or garden bird friendly means making your backyard (or even front yard) more visually interesting, ecologically diverse, and a healthier place for humans, as well.

Invite birds into your yard and you'll be importing natural insect control. Most species do more than their fair share of insect hunting, and many go after some of the worst garden pests. Starlings, for example, can decimate a local Japanese beetle population before the beetles decimate your rose garden. Larger species, such as owls or kestrels, may take care of rodents, such as mice or voles. Fruit eaters spread seeds. Helping birds fosters natural balance and can be a wonderful way to teach children about wild creatures and biology in an easy-to-access backyard laboratory.

Of course, just as a homeowner's house has locks on the doors and windows, a bird is also looking for security. Where you place a birdhouse, feeder, or birdbath is a matter of finding a location that is safe from the many creatures that prey on birds. As beautiful as they are to homeowners, birds and their eggs are attractive food for predators wild and domestic, from snakes to housecats to raccoons.

All that may seem like a lot to consider, but in practice, it really isn't that difficult or complex. It's just a matter of seeing things from a bird's-eye perspective. Establishing a safe and healthy refuge for birds is actually all about common sense and can even be fun.

This book is written specifically to make things as easy as possible. You'll find everything you need to know, from building fun, fanciful, and colorful structures and how best to protect them from the elements and hungry predators that want to make them dinner, to the precise housing size requirements of each species—and much, much more.

Build-It-Yourself Birdhouses begins with a general overview of key topics, including the plants and landscape features that birds favor, their water needs, and how to keep vulnerable winged creatures safe. We've included a chapter on construction basics, covering the best tools and the quickest and easiest techniques for creating sturdy birdhouses and feeders that will not only attract your favorite

This black-capped chickadee has found a home in a post-mounted birdhouse with plenty of clear line-of-sight to detect predators. The house is a simple construction but provides everything this bird needs to nurture the next generation.

species but will also look good in the yard for many seasons to come. You'll find a special section covering fascinating decorating techniques, such as cutting small wood pieces that add massive amounts of personality to any birdhouse. All of these projects and techniques have been developed for the novice craftsperson and relatively inexperienced woodworker. You should be able to build any birdhouse in this book inside of a weekend, if not over a long afternoon. Just don't be surprised if you catch the DIY birding bug and find yourself crafting additional bird structures for friends and family and customizing backyard structures to capture your own personality and tastes.

BEAUTIFUL BIRDHOUSES FOR BEAUTIFUL BIRDS

A CUSTOM, ONE-OF-A-KIND BIRDHOUSE is a yard decoration that serves up two kinds of beauty. The structure itself is your way to add color and form that reflects your taste and your landscape style. But the actual function of the birdhouse means it will attract lively and often colorful accents in the form of fascinating birds. That part of the equation can translate to hours of enjoyment spent watching small, often colorful, living things go about their lives.

Unless you're building it strictly as decoration, any birdhouse you craft has two goals. First, it needs to be a project that will add something to the look of your yard or garden. Second, it must accommodate the needs of the birds you want to attract, which means providing space, comfort, and safety for nesting. If the birdhouse isn't a sanctuary with the right dimensions and placed near essentials such as food and water, birds will find somewhere else to raise their young.

A birdhouse can be a vital replacement for fast-disappearing natural habitats. Cavity-nesting birds—the species that use birdhouses—have fewer nesting options than ever before. The combination of human population spread and climate change continues to deal a harsh blow to the wild places birds have traditionally called home. Humans understandably seek to limit nuisance insect and rodent populations, such as mosquitoes and mice, which are natural food sources for many bird species. Add to that the toxic chemicals we often use to eliminate these pests—chemicals that take their toll on fragile eggs and chicks, as well as adult birds—and it isn't surprising that birds have an increasingly tough time surviving in the modern world.

Building a birdhouse is one small way to help out.

Timing is a key factor to drawing occupants to any birdhouse. Mount your birdhouse *before* the nesting season begins, which—depending on species and where you live—can be as early as late winter. You can also leave a birdhouse up all year.

Birdhouses are generally called nest boxes because they are used over nesting season. But a roost box is left up even in cold months as an emergency shelter for birds caught in bad weather or wintery conditions. Leaving a birdhouse out over winter means dealing with repairs from the extended exposure to the elements. In either case, the birdhouse should be completely clean before nesting birds arrive in the spring.

The "where" is as important as the "when." Mount the birdhouse at the right height (see the chart on page 23) in a spot that receives a good amount of sunshine but not where the sun will shine directly on the front of the house or make the house too hot. Mottled shade is fine, but deep shade is not attractive to birds looking for a nest site. Avoid locations with high winds. And although different birds prefer different surroundings—particulars that are covered in the individual projects that follow—all birds want to nest in a place that is hard for potential predators to reach.

But a birdhouse alone, however well-suited to its intended tenants, won't entice birds into your yard. After all, a birdhouse is where birds will live, procreate, and raise their young. To create the ideal location, you need to understand how birds nest, what they use birdhouses for, and what they look for in the perfect location. Without comfort, safety, food, and water, birds will find somewhere else to raise their young.

LANDSCAPING FOR BIRDS

Enticing feathered travelers to use your carefully crafted and wonderfully showy birdhouse begins with your yard and garden design. The ideal terrain reinforces bird safety, ensures reliable food and water sources are close at hand, and tricks birds into thinking that they are truly in a wild setting. Fortunately for homeowners, the ideal bird landscape is also a healthy, diverse, and beautiful environment that can be as appealing to humans as it is to birds.

Begin with the plants. Plain, manicured lawn offers very little to most birds. That's not to say that you have to rip up all your carefully tended sod, but you will need other plants in the yard to catch a migrating bird's eye. The bonus is that most plants you would incorporate to tempt birds add wonderful colors and forms to the look of any yard.

- **Bushes and shrubs.** Wild birds love almost any plant that produces berries, which means a wide range of bushes and shrubs are ideal for the bird-friendly yard. Obvious choices include blueberry, blackberry, and raspberry. Most gardeners find sharing the crop a fair trade for the company of birds and their lovely songs, but birds' tastes extend beyond those common plants. They will flock to serviceberry, sumac, common juniper, viburnum, holly, elderberry, mulberry, and huckleberry, all of

As the name implies, butterfly bush attracts butterflies . . . and the birds that hunt them.

Some trees, such as maple, spruce, and willow, are custom-made for birds, providing both shelter and fruit other animals rarely touch.

- **Flowers and blooming vines.** Flowers represent a potential feast for birds in the form of nectar, seeds and other edible parts, and the insects and other invertebrates attracted to the blooms. Bird favorites include sunflowers, petunias, trumpet honeysuckle, strawberries, barberries, and trumpet creepers.

- **Ornamental grasses.** A feature in low-maintenance gardens everywhere, ornamental grasses are wonderful, water-conserving landscape options. When they go to seed, birds will happily feast on the seed heads, and many species will use ornamental grass stalks and leaves to line their nests. Favorite grasses include switchgrass, little bluestem, Indian ricegrass, blue fescue, Canada wild rye, and buffalograss.

which can serve as interesting, low-maintenance additions to a bed or shrub border. Other shrubs, such as butterfly bush, lilac, weigela, summersweet, pokeweed, and Rose of Sharon, are bird favorites for the insects they attract. The most alluring shrubs for small birds will be those with loose, open structures that provide plenty of nooks and crannies for vulnerable fliers to rest in safety.

- **Trees.** Birds turn to trees for their protective cover, shade, food (fruit and nuts, as well as insects), and potential nesting sites. It's worth noting that open-nesting bird species will ignore your birdhouse because they create their nests in the branches of their preferred trees. Cavity nesters, however, should find your birdhouse a convenient substitute to searching for just the right vacant natural cavity. Feathered visitors especially enjoy dogwoods, crabapple, cherry (and just about any other fruit tree), American beech, elm, and locust.

The trumpet honeysuckle is just one of many flowering vines that offer a stunning flower display for the homeowner and attract a variety of bird species.

When landscaping for birds, selecting native plant species gives you a leg up on success because they are more likely to thrive in the local climate while requiring less tending and water. Native species are also recognizable to native birds, giving them a sense of comfort that comes from familiar surroundings.

Bird-friendly yard or garden design involves layering. Create different levels of vegetation interspersed with open areas—especially the area around the birdhouse. An open expanse allows birds to see any potential predators long before they strike. When layering plants, don't be afraid to pack them in densely along the edges of the yard to give birds somewhere to hide from hawks and other airborne predators.

If you regularly grow a vegetable garden, you might want to make the modest investment in a roll of bird netting. You can also use the netting to cover any trees, such as a favorite black cherry, that you don't want your feathered friends stripping.

When maintaining your garden, messy equals good where birds are concerned. Don't trim or prune hedges as you normally might, avoid dead-heading, and let plants sprawl. Birds will often eat dead flower heads, and many will gladly use dry plant stems as nest material.

Of course, you also want to keep songbirds as safe as possible. That means avoiding insecticides and herbicides that can quickly impact bird populations. Pay a little more for organic fertilizers and soil conditioners and leave the synthetic-chemical-laden products on the shelf. With their fast metabolism and relatively light body weight, birds quickly succumb to any potential poison.

CATERING TO FLYING DINERS

Bird feeders are natural complements to a bird-house, and the feeders in the last chapter of this book are just as distinctive and stylish as the birdhouses themselves. But feeders are not a substitute for a varied mix of plants and other natural food sources in the yard. Berry bushes, fruit trees, strawberries, and plants, such as sunflowers, that produce easily harvested seeds are all preferred food sources for birds. A wealth of flowering plants will also draw a bounty of insects, which are themselves potential menu items for many bird species. A feeder should supplement rather than be a substitute for all those sources.

Ornamental grasses are stunning fillers for a garden border or bed, and they attract a range of songbirds.

That said, the right bird feeder can add a wonderful visual to the backyard, especially if you choose a distinctive design, such as the Scarecrow Suet Feeder (page 142) or the Zen Tray Feeder (page 152). But feeders also entail responsibilities. If you expect birds to stick around, don't let the feeder go empty. Clean it regularly, and never let the feeder grow moldy or rot. If you're accommodating overwintering birds, make sure you keep the feeder out and stocked year round.

What you put in a bird feeder depends on the species you're feeding. Different foods attract different birds. That's why many backyard birders set out more than one kind of feeder, offering additional mixes that will entice a range of species. But you also have to be practical; cost can be a significant factor when you're filling a feeder on a regular basis. The price of any seed mix is determined not only by the primary seed but also by the amount of filler, such as milo. Here are common bird feed ingredients:

- **Black-oil sunflower seed.** Rich in fats, nutrients, and flavor, these seeds are sold with the hull on because they have a thin shell most birds can easily crack. That means, as with many feeder ingredients, you can expect a mess underneath the feeder (a good reason to place any feeder over a bed of ivy or other ground cover). This is the favorite seed for a wide range of birds, from cardinals to doves to finches. Unfortunately, it's also one of the more expensive bird-feed staples. These large seeds are generally used in hopper, tray, or platform feeders.

- **Cracked corn.** This inexpensive filler draws several birds; doves, quail, sparrows, and ducks will all eat it with gusto. Cracked corn is not especially nutritious, so it shouldn't comprise the majority of feed on offer. Be aware that cracked corn is favorite of squirrels, so it's best used in a squirrel-proof feeder. Or, you can take the tack of many birders and have a dedicated squirrel feeder.

- **Dried fruit.** Few prepackaged seed mixes include dried fruit, but many birds find it a tasty variation in their diet. Smaller edibles, such as raisins and currants, are easy for small species to handle. However, many birds enjoy dried cranberries, blueberries, cherries, and dates. Those treats are especially favored by all types of bluebirds, catbirds, and waxwings. Grapes are another special addition and are relished by grosbeaks, towhees, tanagers, and robins, among others. Many birds will also flock to a cut orange half posted on a feeder so that the birds have access to the juicy flesh of the fruit. Regardless of what fruit you add to a feeder, keep a sharp eye out for any signs of mold or rotting, which can have an adverse affect on bird health.

- **Eggshells.** Although a supplement rather than a food, crushed eggshells are a great addition to any bird feeder. Birds use this type of grit to grind their food in their crops, and eggshells supply crucial calcium. The eggshells must be cleaned and sterilized by baking in an oven for about 15 minutes at 300°F (150°C, or gas mark 2).

- **Mealworms.** The dried larvae of the mealworm beetle are appropriately named because they make an incredibly good source of protein for birds such as chickadees, titmice, bluebirds, and wrens.

- **Millet.** Millet is a round seed preferred by ground feeders, including doves, juncos, and sparrows. Birds who frequent hanging feeders tend to toss out the millet to get to other, tastier parts of the feeder's mix. That's why millet is best used as a ground feed or for low feeders. The millet used as feed is white millet; red millet is even less desirable, and most birds will ignore it.

- **Milo.** An inexpensive red round seed, milo is used as a filler to add weight and volume to bird-feeder mixes. The seed is also called sorghum and is not particularly nutritious or tasty. Most birds actually toss it aside—leading to a mess on the ground and wasted money.

- **Nyjer.** The tiny black seed of the African daisy, Nyjer has a lot of fans in the avian world. It is especially favored by some of the most beautiful songbirds, such as goldfinches and siskins. It's also eaten by seed-eaters with small, pointed bills, including redpolls, juncos, mourning doves, and purple finches. The seed is best used in a feeder with smaller holes so that you don't wind up with a lot of this relatively expensive food scattered over the ground.

- **Peanuts.** As popular with birds as they are with humans, unsalted peanuts are a wonderful, oil-rich addition to the bird feeder. Smaller birds prefer shelled nuts, and any bird will find them easier to get at than working through a shell. The best are raw, organic peanuts, although you can also opt for roasted peanuts as long as they aren't salted or covered with any kind of coating.

- **Pumpkin and squash seed.** Dried pumpkin and squash seeds can be wonderful complements to a bird-feeder mix. High in nutrition and oils, these are perfect as fall food sources to help birds bulk up for the colder months. Many birds will be attracted to the seeds, including house sparrows, blue jays, chickadees, northern cardinals, titmice, and nuthatches. However, don't feed birds seasoned or salted pumpkin seeds.

- **Safflower seed.** This seed, cultivated by humans for its oil, is also an excellent bird food. High in protein and fat, it can be a great choice for feeders where grackles, blackbirds, or squirrels are a problem because those troublesome food stealers don't like safflower seeds. Finches, chickadees, titmice, grosbeaks, and even cardinals find the seed delectable. Because of its widespread availability, safflower is a relatively inexpensive addition to a bird-feeder mix.

- **Striped sunflower seed.** Striped sunflower seeds—much like black-oil sunflower seeds—are a natural favorite of most birds. Bird-feeder mixes can include sunflower seeds hulled or not, but hulled seeds make far less of a mess under the feeder. These are also a favorite of squirrels, so if you use them in your feeder, make sure there is some protection against furry food stealers.

The bird-feeder mix you buy or make will depend on the diet of the birds you're hoping to attract, as well as that of other native species. Consult your local agricultural extension office or Audubon chapter for advice on which foods work best in your area. Be prepared to open your wallet; the best (meaning, the oiliest and most nutritious) seed and feeder mixes can be expensive—especially if you're successful and attract a diversity of long-term, hungry avian visitors. Most bird lovers look at the money spent as similar to vet bills for a family pet: an inherent cost for something you love.

Where you're dealing with many different bird species, plan on putting out different types of feeders. Different designs are meant to service different types of birds. Regardless of what type you use, you absolutely must ensure that the feeder

NOT IN THE DIET!

The following items are not recommended for birds or bird feeders:

- Chocolate chips—or any other chocolate
- Baked goods of any kind
- Potato chips
- Bread

A flock of cedar waxwings enjoys a sun-drenched birdbath full of clean, cool water.

does [...]
Bir[...]
wo[...]
st[...]
t[...]
[...]

[...] t a
[...] ng

birds [...] re is
a local pond, stream [...] ay
serve the purpose for any avian [...] ost
cases, though, it's a good idea to provide water.

- **Birdbaths.** Despite the name, a birdbath serves *two* uses: as a source of (hopefully) clean drinking water as well as a place for birds to clean themselves. The second function complicates the first. Splashing in the bath is a way for birds to remove both dust and parasites, such as mites. Dirty birdbath water can spread diseases among a local bird population. That's why birdbath water should be changed entirely at least once a week and ideally more often. In fact, pros recommend cleaning a birdbath at least twice a week during the nesting season. A full cleaning requires more than just dumping out the existing water. You should be ready to scrub out the birdbath—wearing rubber gloves to protect your own health. Use a warm water-and-bleach solution, rinsing well and allowing the birdbath to dry completely before refilling it with clean, cool water. Never simply top off a birdbath.

  Placement affects whether birds actually use a birdbath and how easy it is to clean. It should be positioned in full or partial shade to limit the growth of algae. Don't place a feeder directly above the birdbath or you'll have even more of a mess on your hands when cleaning time comes. Lastly, consider safety: both you and the birds should have a clear view in all directions to detect any predators.

- **Bird ponds.** This is your opportunity to add an incredible landscape feature and provide an excellent source of water for birds. A ground-level pond is a completely doable weekend project, and you'll find complete installation kits at home centers, nurseries, and online. The kits usually include a filter and recirculation pump, and some even come with a fountain feature. A bird pond differs from more traditional backyard ponds in size and depth. It is usually modest in proportions— no more than 3 feet (0.9 m) in diameter—and it should not be deeper than 2½ inches (6.4 cm) to ensure bird safety. Birds prefer a matte surface that they can easily grip, so avoid slick plastic and

This sparrow is in the thrall of a birdbath fountain. Water in motion is endlessly attractive to all bird species.

choose rubberized pond liners instead. You might also allow dirt around the pond to become muddy, because certain species, such as robins, swallows, and martins, use mud to build their nests.

- **Moving water.** As much as they love a good source of clean, fresh water, birds are even more drawn to moving water. Waterfalls, gurgling brooks, and the sound of dripping water slowly making its way over rocks are all enticing to a bird. Adding a modest waterfall to a bird pond can be an incredible alluring feature to all kinds of wild birds, but you can also add a dripper or mister to a birdbath for a similar effect.

THE SAFE SANCTUARY

Food and water aren't of much use if the birdhouse and your yard don't offer a safe environment for vulnerable small birds. The unfortunate truth is that the world is a dangerous place for many wild birds. It might seem like the power of flight provides a lot of protection, but every bird must rest and build a nest. Any nesting site becomes a prime target for a range of predators. Some attack the birds, others want the eggs and nestlings, and some adversaries are just looking to take over the nest. A few target all of the above. Understanding the dangers birds face from predators wild and domestic is the first step in protecting them from those dangers.

- **Pets.** A family pet can be the first and most persistent threat to backyard birds. Although many don't present a predatory danger, dogs think birds are play toys; from the bird's perspective, a dog is just another fast-moving enemy. That's why it's best to keep your dog on a short leash if you're hoping to attract birds. Cats—both house cats allowed outdoors and feral felines—represent a more deadly threat. A 2013 joint study by the Smithsonian's Conservation Biology Institute and the United States Fish and Wildlife Institute found that cats kill billions of birds each year. Whether you have a hungry domesticated tabby or your neighborhood hosts a small population of wild cats, a combination of predator guards and careful landscaping are the best protection against cat attacks. Clear any brush or obstruction under and around the birdhouse and bird feeder so that cats don't have a concealed avenue from which to stalk birds. Neutering house cats can also help curb their hunting instincts, and outdoor cat enclosures can be a great way for house cats to enjoy viewing the birds without harming them.

- **Squirrels.** Although birds have little to fear from squirrels, the rodents can be competitors for available food. Squirrels will rarely attack a bird's nest unless there are no other food sources available—in which case eggs become a reasonable dinner. But squirrels look at bird feeders as a free lunch buffet, which is why your feeder should have a squirrel-proofing feature if you have squirrels in your yard. As an alternative, you can put out a squirrel feeder. (Just keep in mind that doesn't necessarily mean they will limit themselves to their own feeder.)

A combination of predator guards and careful landscaping are the best protection against cat attacks.

- **Snakes.** Snakes are a more serious threat to birds, nestlings, and eggs alike. These slithering predators are silent and can fit through amazingly small spaces. Although they are more prevalent in southern states, it's smart to investigate what snakes are active in your region. You can block access with several different types of birdhouse guards, but be careful that the guard leaves no spaces through which an enterprising snake could pass. You can also trap a snake and remove it to a distant wild area, although chances are another will take its place.

- **Raccoons.** A primary bird predator, raccoons are clever, always hungry, and incredibly persistent. Generally nocturnal feeders, raccoons will attack birds, eggs, and nestlings in their birdhouse, usually by reaching in and grabbing whatever they can. They will also ravage bird feeders given half a chance. Raccoons are repeat offenders who return often to the scene of the crime, remembering where they scored on a previous visit. The secret to protecting birds from raccoons is to prevent the raccoons from ever reaching the birdhouse or feeder. Baffles on tree trunks or birdhouse mounting posts are highly effective in deterring raccoons. Entry hole guards are a secondary line of defense in those cases where the raccoon can find its way around a baffle. Hole guards should extend the entry hole by 6 inches (15.2 cm) or more—the average reach of a raccoon.

- **Predatory birds.** Depending on the species of bird you hope to entice into your yard, the bird may be preyed on by several other types of winged foe. Purple martins, for instance, may be hunted or harassed by blue jays, crows, owls, starlings, and raptors. The entry hole and birdhouse itself become a protective sanctuary for prey birds. It's why you won't find any perches on the birdhouses in this book; they can serve as a resting place for predatory birds looking to get at the birds and eggs inside. Size doesn't matter when it comes to predatory and aggressive bird species; small starlings are one of the most obnoxious bird enemies. Introduced to the United States in 1890, this nonnative aggressor has proliferated throughout the country. Starlings not only take over existing nests—including those in birdhouses you've put out—they also destroy other species' eggs and nestlings in the process. Starlings try to dominate bird feeders as well. Combatting them involves eliminating perches on feeders, using black-oil sunflower seeds (which the starlings can't crack), and using unstable feeders that twirl and won't allow the starling to land. Larger predatory birds are harder to defend against. The best defense against something like a hawk or other predator is to provide plenty of open shrubs or tightly formed trees where smaller songbirds can hide.

Once you've established a bird-friendly landscape, planned for providing food and water, and made the area as predator-proof as possible, it's time to tackle building the ideal birdhouse.

PREDATOR GUARDS

Homeowners can choose from a number of ways to protect birdhouse residents. Most are very low cost, and none take a lot of effort. Each works best for a certain type of predator. The most basic includes greasing a pole on which the birdhouse is mounted or nailing long carpet tack strips vertically to the post. Obviously, the former works best on metal or plastic support posts and the latter on wood. Here are other solutions:

Roof. Extending the roof several inches makes it much more difficult for squirrels, raccoons, or house cats to get at the entry hole and reach inside. The bonus is that a longer roof plane provides more shade, keeping nestlings and adult birds cooler during the hottest part of the day.

Tree or post baffles. A simple metal or plastic sleeve wrapped *completely* around a tree trunk or birdhouse mounting post will deter many predators, such as raccoons and snakes, from climbing up to the nest. Ideally, this type of baffle should be at least 24 inches wide. Use a removeable baffle on a tree trunk, as the tree may otherwise be damaged or killed as it grows.

Noel guard. Named for Jim Noel, the avid bird conservationist who invented it, the Noel guard is a squared-off tunnel of wire mesh attached directly in front of the entry hole on a birdhouse and extending 5 inches or more out from the hole. The guard is highly effective at deterring predation by raccoons, cats, and large birds, such as hawks.

Cone baffle. This is one of the most effective predator guards when used correctly. The baffle is shaped just like the cone that is wrapped around a pet's neck after surgery. It is best suited for a circular post or uniform tree trunk, although it can be adapted for use on a squared-off post. The collar blocks snakes, raccoons, cats, and squirrels from climbing all the way up the tree or post to get to the birdhouse. The

Noel guard *Hole extender*

collar must be snugly secured around the post or tree to ensure a predator can't slip into a space between the inner ring and the post or tree trunk. Any collar must also be wide enough to deter climbing around the lip—which usually translates to at least 30 inches in diameter. Collars can be plastic or exterior grade metal, such as coated zinc.

Stovepipe baffle. Used exclusively on posts, a stovepipe baffle is a complicated predator guard that is fixed on the inside mounting apparatus, with a moving outer pipe. Climbing predators will have a difficult go of it because the baffle is slick and hard to hold and spins whenever a climber tries to get a purchase. Snakes, however, can climb up the center space.

Hole extender. There are various styles of hole extenders, but all function on the same principle of lengthening the space through which predators, such as larger birds, squirrels, cats, and raccoons, have to reach into the birdhouse to harass adult birds or grab eggs or nestlings. You can purchase prefab versions under the brand name Bird Guardian, but you can easily make your own by screwing a wood block that has been drilled with a hole to match the entry hole right over the existing entry hole. Or, attach a PVC flange and length of PVC pipe the next available size up from the birdhouse entry hole size so that the pipe sticks straight out.

BIRDHOUSE CONSTRUCTION BASICS

A BIRDHOUSE IS NOT AN OVERLY DIFFICULT STRUCTURE to craft. Even larger nest boxes require only modest skills and a small amount of wood and fasteners. You might be a novice DIYer and inexperienced woodworker, but that's okay. You'll still be able to tackle any project in this book as long you bring a little patience and attention to detail to the effort.

For the most part, the steps in the projects require basic versions of sawing, drilling, and joining. The only somewhat challenging requirement is cutting edge bevels and angles. However, if you have a good speed square and the right saw—an adjustable table saw or miter saw—even beveled rip cuts won't frustrate you.

If you're a little more experienced and like to modify designs and plans, feel free to change any of the projects in this book. However, always check the bird species sizing chart on page 23 for correct dimensions. Although birds in the wild don't carry a ruler, these specifications are a good baseline to maintain—especially the size of the entry hole. It's okay to put your own personal flair on any birdhouse design, but the goal remains to make a given species comfortable in the structure over a nesting season (unless you're using the birdhouse for purely decorative reasons—in which case, go wild).

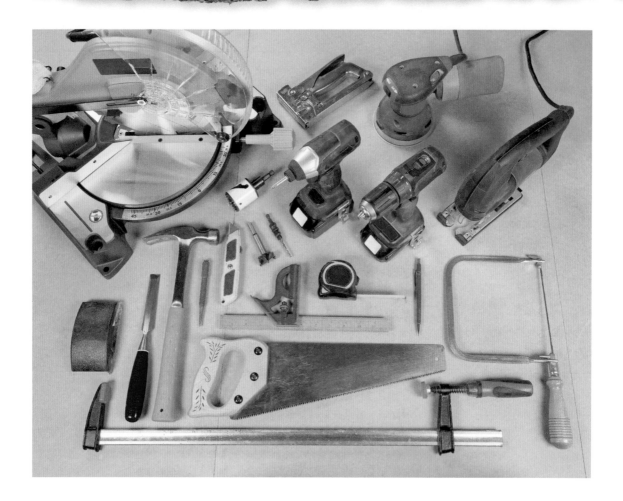

THE TOOLS YOU'LL NEED

Small projects such as birdhouses don't require a workshop full of tools. In fact, most of what you need you probably already have in your garage. The good news is that working with such small, simple projects means you'll have the option in many cases to use inexpensive hand tools in place of any power tools you may not own.

• **Saws.** A *table saw* will quickly make all the cuts necessary to create almost all of the projects in this book (except for small, decorative accents). The same can be said for the more mobile and less expensive *miter saw*. A *circular saw* may be appropriate for many of the cuts and can be used in combination with jigs to make beveled cuts. In any case, choosing the right blade will make the whole process go more smoothly and lead to a more satisfactory result. The most efficient blade will be a 50-tooth general purpose or combination blade. In a few instances, a *jigsaw* will be necessary to cut intricate shapes.

Options: Are you a purist who likes to work with nothing more powerful than elbow grease? You can feasibly construct this book's projects using general handsaws, such as a *panel saw*. But you will need two—a crosscut and a rip cut saw. A *coping saw* can do the job of a jigsaw with less expense, albeit much more slowly. (However, "slower" can translate to "more control" for inexperienced woodworkers.) Woodworking saws, such as a *Dozuki* or a *dovetail saw*, can be handy for more intricate cuts in nicer woods, where you want the cut to be very clean and precise for aesthetic as well as assembly reasons.

- **Power drill and bit set.** There's really no excuse not to own a *cordless power drill* and range of bits. The most common size for a home craftsman is ⅜ inch. A full set including drill, bits, extra battery, and a batter-proof carrying case won't break the bank. Extras, such as a *drill-bit depth gauge*, are extremely handy.

  Options: None.

- **Specialty drill bits.** Drilling entry holes can be done precisely and quickly with one of several specialty drill bits. *Forstner bits* are specifically designed to cut clean, precise through-holes in fine woodworking, and they're the desired tool for making birdhouse entry holes. The bit minimizes tearing and produces a clean inside edge.

  Options: A Forstner bit set can be a little pricey. If you prefer, you can buy a single *spade bit* for the entry hole in the size you need, but be aware that spade bits tend to produce tear-out and a rougher hole than a Forstner bit. Work slowly and carefully and make sure the spade bit is sharp before you begin. (You'll still need to sand the inside edge of the hole.) A *hole saw* is perhaps the crudest tool you can choose for drilling entry holes, and it makes for a rough inside edge that will need to be sanded smooth. Hole saws also generally have ½ inch tangs, which means the bit won't fit in a ⅜ inch drill.

- **Tape measure.** A high-quality tape measure is an absolute necessity for any household toolbox. Just keep in mind that a tape measure is only as good as the attention you give it—always measure twice and cut once.

Options: A 3- or 4-foot *metal straight edge* is a little harder to maneuver than a tape measure but is very precise and offers the bonus of an edge you can use to trace straight lines.

- **Sander.** Thanks to the small size of most of these birdhouses, there really is no need for a power sander to do the necessary cleanup work. However, if you have a *palm sander*, any sanding you need to do will go much more quickly and with far less effort.

  Option: For the projects in this book, you'll be fine with a simple sanding block and sheets of 80- or 100-grit sandpaper.

THE BEST WOOD

The wood you choose for the birdhouse depends on how exposed the birdhouse will be, how much abuse it will take, the finished appearance you want, and—last but certainly not least—expense.

- **Softwoods.** Softwoods are less expensive, lighter weight, and easier to fabricate with than hardwoods. However, not all softwoods are appropriate for exterior applications such as a birdhouse. The best for outdoor structures are those that are naturally resistant to the elements and insects: redwood, cedar, and cypress. For small structures such as a birdhouse, cedar is the best choice.

- **Hardwoods.** Turn to hardwoods for absolute durability and where looks really matter to you. If you're placing the birdhouse in a highly visible location and don't plan on painting it, using a hardwood, such as cherry or walnut, might make sense. Although these woods are considerably more expensive than softwood options, they won't break the bank in a structure that is so modest in size. Keep in mind that hardwoods are going to be somewhat more difficult to craft, especially if you're using hand tools.

- **Plywood.** Plywood is an inexpensive and durable choice for a birdhouse, but you have to choose the right plywood for the application. Obviously, any plywood you use for a birdhouse must be exterior grade, such as CDX. Generally, to ensure the integrity of the structure, no plywood thinner than ½ inch is used. For an extremely handsome appearance, you can use the slightly more expensive exterior-rated Baltic birch plywood or birch-veneer versions. In any case, it's best to avoid plywood with edge voids—or plan on filling the edges with wood putty and sanding them smooth.

Whenever you choose wood for a birdhouse, select the highest grade you can afford and look for clear wood—without knots or other imperfections and with no visible warping or cupping. In constructing the birdhouse, ensure longevity by planning for the wood grain to always run in the longest direction and preferably vertically in the finished piece. End grain and cut ends should be kept out of the potential flow of water as much as feasible.

THE ESSENTIALS

Regardless of the wood you use to build it, certain features are essential in any habitable birdhouse.

Ventilation. Birds not only use a birdhouse as lodging but, in most cases, as a nest site to raise their young. Fresh air for both adults and nestlings is essential. Ventilation gaps or holes not only ensure a free flow of clean air; they help keep the temperature inside the box relatively cool.

Drainage. Drainage holes in the bottom of the birdhouse help remove any unwanted or unhealthy moisture or condensation, but they also facilitate airflow in conjunction with the spaces or holes drilled at the tops of the walls. An alternative to ¼-inch drainage holes is to clip the corners of any birdhouse floor that is recessed inside the walls.

Fasteners. You can nail a birdhouse together, but frankly, birdhouses should be usable for several years. That means screws are the better choice. And, given the exposure, you should always use galvanized, zinc-plated, or stainless steel screws and hardware to prevent corrosion, rust, and fastener failure. Those same finishes will protect hinges, latches, screw eyes, and hanging chain you might use to hang the house or create a cleanout door. Although glue may not be considered a fastener per se, waterproof wood glue is one more way to make sure that birdhouse joints don't allow water to infiltrate the structure.

FINISHING TOUCHES

Most often, birdhouses are left unfinished for two reasons. First, the look of the birdhouse doesn't really matter to a bird. The second reason is that it's just easier not to worry about finishing a

BIRDHOUSE SPECIES SIZING

SPECIES	ENTRY HOLE	HOLE TO GROUND	HOLE TO FLOOR	ROOF TO HOLE	FLOOR DIMENSIONS
American Kestrel	3"	12–30'	9–12"	3"	10 × 12"
American Robin	*	8–10'	*	*	5 × 8"
Bluebird	1½"	4–8'	6–10"	2"	4 × 4"
Chickadee (all species)	1⅛"	7–12'	6–8"	2"	4 × 4"
Flicker	2½"	12–20'	14–16"	16–18	7 × 7"
Flycatcher	1¾"	5–15'	8–10"	2–3"	6 × 6"
House Finch	2"	8–12'	4–6"	2–4"	6 × 6"
House Wren	1–1⅛"	4–10'	3–6"	2"	4 × 4"
Nuthatch	1¼"	5–15'	6–8"	2–4"	4 × 4"
Owl, Barn	4"	10–25'	4– 6"	4–6"	20 × 10"
Owl, Barred	7–10"	15–20'	12–14"	0–4"	14 × 14"
Owl, Screech	3"	10–30"	9–12"	3–5"	9 × 9"
Purple Martin	2⅛"	10–20'	1–1½"	5"	6 × 6"
Sparrow	1 3/16–2"	8–15'	6–7"	3–5"	5 × 5"
Titmouse	1¼"	6–15'	6–8"	2"	4 × 4"
Tree Swallow	1½"	10–15'	5"	1–4"	5 × 5"
Wood Duck	3 × 4"	6–20'	10–12"	4–6"	9 × 9"
Woodpecker	2"	12–20'	10–12"	3–5"	6 × 6"

*Birds are open, ledge nesters. No hole needed.

birdhouse—it's one less step in the construction process. However, many people mount a birdhouse in clear view from a patio, deck, or the back windows of a house. In a well-designed landscape, a birdhouse is a way to accent the look of the yard and garden, and an unfinished structure might not fit into the look you're after.

If you've built a structure entirely of plywood, finishing the surface can be a way of preserving the birdhouse, especially any edges that serve as common points of moisture infiltration. You can use a clear finish as long as it's a low- or no-VOC (volatile organic compound), oil-based, exterior-rated product. You can also stain the wood or even paint it if you so choose. Lighter, more natural shades are preferable. It's usually best to stay away from bright red, which can be a warning color to birds. Darker colors can hold heat from sunlight and make the interior of the birdhouse overly hot. Speaking of the interior, it is no place for a finish of any kind. Carefully limit any finish you use to the exterior surfaces of the birdhouse.

SPECIAL SECTION

CRAFTING THE FINE POINTS

Adding charm to any birdhouse can be a simple matter of decorating what are generally pretty bland outer surfaces. There are lots of ways to pretty up a birdhouse, and the techniques themselves are your gateway to personalizing whatever structure you build.

Cutting Decorative Wood Shapes

Applying wood shapes, such as a faux chimney or gingerbread trim, to the base structure of a birdhouse is one of the most effective ways to customize the look to your tastes. Although this technique takes time and patience, it can make for a one-of-a-kind look that can be a focal part of a yard or garden.

Depending on the intricacy of the shape, you can tape tracing paper over a piece of wood and use the shape on the paper as a cut line (more detailed, curving shapes) or just draw the design directly onto the wood. However, using tracing paper gives you a chance to adjust a flowing freehand design more easily.

Cutting an intricate design out of piece of standard wood is best done with a scroll saw. If you don't want to make the investment in this specialty saw, you may be able to find a scroll saw for rent at a local tool rental store. Otherwise, you can use a rotary tool fit with a router collar and spiral cutting bit to cut out the design. Just be aware that, depending on the thickness of the wood, it may take a lot longer to cut with a rotary and the results are likely to be a lot rougher—requiring a lot of sanding to smooth out. If you're comfortable and experienced with a jigsaw, you can try cutting the shape with that useful tool. As a hand-powered fallback, turn to a coping saw. Just be ready to put

Decorating a birdhouse can be the most fun part of building one, and it's the perfect stage for children to add their own creativity.

a lot of elbow grease and time into even a small decorative shape.

For smaller, more finicky pieces, such as gingerbread, railings, and faux doors or windows, balsa wood is the birdhouse crafter's decorative material of choice. The best thickness for this kind of work is ⅛-inch balsa wood, and you can find packages of balsa wood pieces in any craft or hobby store. Used for model building, these are often the perfect size for architectural embellishments on your birdhouse.

Painting & Texturing

Paint and paint effects are two of the best ways to make a birdhouse stand out in the landscape and visually pop against a background of plant life. Fortunately, birds aren't deterred by most of the colors you might choose. As long as the lodgings are comfortable, convenient, and safe, they don't much care how their housing looks.

Two ironclad rules about applying finishes to a birdhouse are: the material must be nontoxic and it must **only** be applied to exterior surfaces. Ideally, buy low- or no-VOC paints, stains, or finishes, which won't release gases that could be toxic to birds. The projects in this book all call for nontoxic exterior paints, stains, and finishes.

Any crafting store will offer several specialized nontoxic paints or paint additives to create unusual looks. These range from crackled paint, to antiquing finishes, and more. It's best if these effects are limited to surfaces the birds generally won't touch.

You can also use all the paint effects you might use in your home. Distress the outside to create the illusion of an aged cottage or sponge a mottled effect to help the birdhouse blend in with its surroundings. Dilute paint for a whitewashed appearance or even flick the brush at the surface to create a one-of-kind speckled look that mimics the appearance of many songbird eggs.

You don't have to rely on specialized crafting products for a unique finish. Personalizing the look of your birdhouse can be as simple as using thick, visible brushstrokes or taping off sections to paint stripes or geometric shapes in different colors.

Stencils are a great way to add a distinctive element, not only to this birdhouse, but most others as well.

Birdhouse Stenciling

If you're talented enough to paint freehand elements, such as flowers, bees, grass, or lettering, on your birdhouse, then embellishing the design won't be a problem for you. For the rest of us, adding these sorts of painted or stained decorative elements will most likely mean using stencils.

You'll find florals, leaves, abstracts, patterns such as honeycomb and lace, and much, much more at large craft stores, some hardware stores and home centers, and, of course, online. The most basic of these are letter and number cutouts that allow you print messages, single words, or even a street address on the birdhouse. But that's just the tip of the iceberg of the potential stencils represent. You can paint ivy growing up the side of the house to accent a naturalistic style or color scheme. Pattern the roof, sides, front, or all of the birdhouse in a simple geometric or more froufrou lacy pattern. The sky—and your imagination—is the limit when it comes to using, combining, or customizing stencils for the birdhouse.

DECORATIVE ROOFING

Use paint chips to create a specialized surface appearance, such as bricks. Simply cut out the painted sample squares on the chip and then overlap them as you would on a real roof. Use an outdoor crafting glue, such as Mod Podge, to apply the chips to the surface and each other and when you're finished, spray the entire surface with a nontoxic, oil-based clear sealer.

CLASSIC SMALL BIRDHOUSES

BIRDERS HAVE BEEN BUILDING HOMES for their feathered friends for a very long time. It was only natural that eventually certain shapes and styles would become favorites for both the enthusiasts and the birds. You can call them classic in the sense that the basic underpinnings of these designs work time and time again because avid birders and conservationists developed them through trial and error. All of these constructions are ideally suited to lodging the small birds for which they are named.

But because the focus is on unique and handsome designs, this chapter features wonderful variations on those more traditional base designs. You'll find lots of custom touches, along with directions for personalizing the structures even more, to suit your own particular sense of style. You can use the foundations of these structures as launch pads for wherever your imagination will take you. Or, just build them as described for exceptionally eye-catching backyard standouts.

Whatever the case, the keys to success in these projects are simplicity and visual power. Small details, or the right paint in the right place, provide that spark that really draws the eye — without the need for a lot of technical woodwork or specialized tools and materials. Each of these creations has its own special character and ornamentations, which makes building them as much fun as displaying them.

CLASSIC BLUEBIRD HOUSE

This fun and colorful box reflects the intended occupants. It has a long, pleasing shape, streamlined but still architecturally interesting. The project features a flat roof that makes for easy construction but is also perfect for keeping adult birds and their nestlings safe, warm, and dry. A few simple embellishments on the traditional Gilbertson box bring this design to life and make it a unique feature in your backyard, one that's sure to draw compliments from cookout guests.

Bluebirds are some of the most beautiful birds to attract into a backyard, and they produce amazingly beautiful music. Fortunately, regardless of where you live, you'll likely be able to attract bluebirds. The three species each inhabit different, overlapping ranges. The eastern bluebird spreads from the East Coast, west almost to the Rockies, and down from the mid-Atlantic region throughout the southeast to the gulf of Mexico; the mountain bluebird's range extends up through the mountain states, stretching from Mexico to Alaska; and the western bluebird can be found up and down the West Coast and in Arizona, Texas, and Mexico.

The right nest box will not only attract flashes of cerulean flair and explosions of birdsong, it will also do a big favor to the bluebird population at large. Bluebirds were decimated throughout much of the 1960s and 1970s due to habitat destruction and increased competition for nesting sites. Thankfully, the tireless efforts of conservationists and bird lovers led to a rebound. Mounting and maintaining a bluebird box (or boxes) is a great way to keep that positive trend moving in the right direction.

Bluebirds are a meek species and are subject to attack by a variety of predators. Enemies include snakes, raccoons, cats, and even squirrels, but bluebirds are also targeted by house sparrows and

Eastern bluebird

Western bluebird

Mountain bluebird

starlings. A house sparrow will brazenly take over a bluebird nest, evicting or killing the occupants without hesitation. The bluebird's vulnerability is why an entry-hole predator guard would be especially welcome on this house (see page 18).

Face the birdhouse away from prevailing winds, ideally close to low-lying fences or open-form shrubs where the birds can safely perch. Those landscape features give the bluebirds a good vantage point from which to see predators and detect insects. Plan on setting the birdhouse out in late March or early April, depending on how cold it is. You'll want them to have lodgings available for nesting as early as possible.

This structure includes the simplest of hinged openings, involving two brads holding a side wall. This is an essential feature because if you don't maintain the house, the birds will abandon it and not return. Remove old nests and clean the box once youngsters have fledged. More importantly, check the box weekly during windless, rainless days and mild temperatures. Open the door carefully and quickly look inside box to ensure all is well. Don't worry about spooking your lodgers; bluebirds are tolerant of humans, and a human scent won't put them off the birdhouse. However, don't check the box when chicks are more than twelve days old; they could leave the box and die in the open. Check that no invasive bird species have taken over the birdhouse. If they have,

evict the invaders. Make sure you close the hinged side and secure it in place after inspection or cleaning.

This birdhouse is simple in construction. Perhaps the most challenging sections are the decorative wings. Should they prove to be a bit above your pay grade, you can always substitute another nail-on design, such as a large triangle or your own design. Regardless of how you accent it, the house shouldn't take more than a day to build. All the pieces can be cut from a single board, and no special tools are required. Even the angled cuts and beveled edges are basic enough that most anyone with a miter saw and a little patience can execute them perfectly.

OPTING FOR OVAL

Eastern bluebirds are one of several bird species that actually prefer oval entry holes to round ones. This plan design incorporates a round hole for ease of construction, but if you're willing to do a little extra work, cut a 1⅜ inches tall × 2¼ inches wide oval for eastern bluebirds. Just be sure to make the hole those exact dimensions to reduce the possibility of starlings co-opting the house.

TOOLS & MATERIALS

Tape measure

1 × 6 × 6" cedar board

Carpenter's pencil

Table or circular saw

Jigsaw or coping saw

Sandpaper

Miter saw

Power drill & bits

C-clamp

1⅜" Forstner bit

2" deck screws

Waterproof wood glue

Hammer

Finish brads

Exterior clear finish

Paintbrush

Exterior gloss white paint

Exterior gloss blue paint

Putty knife

Wood putty

Nailset

CUT LIST

(2) ¾ × 4 × 10¾" sides

(1) ¾ × 5½ × 9¾" front

(1) ¾ × 5½ × 14½" back

(1) ¾ × 4 × 4" floor

(1) ¾ × 5½ × 8½" roof

(2) ¾ × 3 × 3½" wings

HOW TO BUILD A
A CLASSIC BLUEBIRD HOUSE

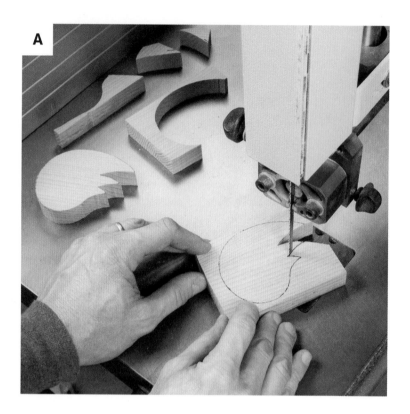

A

1 Cut all the pieces for the birdhouse from a single cedar board (see the cutting diagram page 156).

Note: Although most 1x boards are a uniform ¾" thick, it's wise to dry fit and adjust pieces individually to accommodate any variations in thickness.

2 Trace a wing on a 3 × 3½" wing blank (see diagram on page 156). Cut the wing shape out using a jigsaw or coping saw [**fig. A**]. Sand the cut edges, and then use the cut wing as a template to outline the second wing. Cut out the second wing as you did the first, and sand the edges.

B

3 Drill ¼" drainage holes in a cross pattern on the floor. Bevel one end of the front and back to 14°. Orient the bevel so that the rough faces will be inside the birdhouse. Cut a 14° angle in one end of each side [**fig. B**].

4 Measure and mark 6½" up from the bottom of the front wall, centering the mark side to side. Clamp the front to a work surface on top of a piece of scrap wood. Drill a 1½" hole centered on the mark using a Forstner bit [**fig. C**].

5 Clamp the floor to a work surface. Position one wall side along one edge of the floor and check that it is flush. Drill pilot holes and glue and screw the side to the floor with 2" deck screws. Drill pilot holes and glue and screw the front to the floor and to the front edge of the side wall.

C

6 Position the back so that the top of the back is exactly ¼" higher than the side. Check that the roof sits flat across the edge bevels of the front and back and leave a ¼ " gap along the side for ventilation. When you're satisfied that the back is properly positioned, drill pilot holes and glue and nail it to the side and floor [**fig. D**].

7 Dry fit the second side wall between the front and back, exactly ¼" below the tops of the back and front. Check that it moves somewhat freely between the two (if necessary, sand down the edges). Measure and mark pilot holes exactly 9" up from the bottom of the side wall on either edge. Transfer the marks to the front and back. Drill pilot holes through the front and back into the edges of the side wall. Drive brads into the holes. Check that the side wall hinges open properly [**fig. E**].

8 Drill a hole 1" up from the bottom, through the front or rear face and into the edge of the hinged side. Slide a dowel or small screw into the hole to lock the side closed.

9 Paint the wings gloss white and the roof light blue. Place putty over all the screw heads in the body as desired and sand smooth. Finish the birdhouse body with a clear, no-VOC finish, if desired. Position the roof and drill pilot holes down into the tops of the front and back. Glue and screw the roof in place.

10 Measure and mark horizontal and vertical centerlines on both side walls using a grease pencil or other permanent marker. Center a wing on one sidewall and mark the edges with key marks corresponding to the centerlines [**fig. F**]. Transfer the key marks to the edges of the second wing.

11 Align one wing and drill two pilot holes along its midline. Nail the wing to the side wall with brads. Repeat with the second wing. Use a nailset to sink the brads. Touch up the paint over the nail heads.

12 Fasten the birdhouse to a tree, post, fence, or other structure with screws driven through the back tongue that extends below the birdhouse. The house should be 4 to 8" off the ground.

FOLLOWING THE TRAIL

Bluebird activists and conservationists have developed a strategy for ensuring the health of this songbird's population across the country. Called *bluebird trails*, the strategy involves setting out bluebird nesting boxes in a series along a defined route. This spurs bluebirds to use the boxes again and again, becoming comfortable with the location. Key to the success of any bluebird trail is the proper habitat. They are best set up in rural areas with scattered trees and light or no ground cover. The ideal habitat has fence lines, wires, or low, open tree branches from which the birds can spot and hunt insects. The boxes should be at least 50" from wooded or brush-strewn areas and should be kept at least 100 yds apart for western and eastern bluebirds and at least 200 yds apart for mountain bluebirds.

THE BAT CAVE

The right bat house can bring a whole new definition of cool to your yard, outbuilding, or house. And this particular design redefines hip, with a matte black exterior and outlined bat shape on the front that capture the mystery forever surrounding this nocturnal creature.

Of course, bats aren't birds; they're winged mammals (the only mammal who can truly fly!). Bats are just as beneficial for your yard, garden, and personal comfort as any bird could be. They are keystone ecological actors who vacuum up insects, including some of the most annoying, such as mosquitos. They also prey on incredibly damaging agricultural pests such as corn earworm moth. In fact, some estimates peg the real-dollar agricultural industry benefits of bat insect control at hundreds of millions of dollars every year. Larger bats, known as megabats, eat both fruit and insects, while smaller microbats tend to feed exclusively on small insects.

They serve other important ecological purposes as well. They are pollinators in many environments where pollinators are few and far between. They spread seed far and wide, and bat waste—known as guano—is an amazingly rich and nutritious soil fertilizer. And free!

A bat house such as the one in this project must provide a suitable home for at least a small colony of bats. These are social creatures who nest together, so any bat house will be larger than a birdhouse. Bats are also more finicky about where they lodge, so placement and orientation will be even more important with a bat house than with a birdhouse.

Start with your property. Bats require a ready source of clean water. If you don't have a pond, stream, or some fairly large, constant source of clean water within 1,500 feet (457.2 meters), bats will likely not stay there. You should also have a diverse landscape that draws a lot of insects.

Although the house in this project has been kept simple, it would be reasonable to double the thickness of the house and incorporate a front and back cavity. You can also use multiple houses placed next to one another.

Mount this house 12 to 20 feet (3.7 to 6.1 m) above the ground. Many people mount bat houses on wood poles because it's an easy way to put the house where you want it, but post mounting is not ideal. Preferably, fasten bat houses on the side of a house or shed, near the eaves. Or, attach it to a barn where the bats might naturally roost. Place the bat house as close to small potential entry points of the larger structure as possible; that way, bats will be more likely to detect and use the opening of the bat house. Mount the house in early spring, before the bats come out of hibernation.

Bats like to be warm. Any bat house should receive 6 to 8 hours of direct sun a day, and the ideal internal temperature of the house is a stable and constant 80 to 95°F (27 to 35°C). Ideally, the bat house should face east, southeast, or south. In warmer areas of the country, the house can be finished natural, painted a light color, or left unfinished. Where nights get cool in the summer, at least the top half of the house should be painted a darker color: gray for fair temperature climates or black where the nights are much colder than the days. This dramatic design is decorated for cooler climes.

HOT HOUSE

This south-facing wall of a stucco building is just about the ideal location for a bat house; the surface slowly releases heat after the sun goes down, ensuring the bat house stays warm through the night.

TOOLS & MATERIALS

Tape measure

½" exterior grade plywood

Carpenter's pencil

Circular saw

Miter saw

Roll of fiberglass window screen

Shears

Staple gun

80-grit sandpaper

Staples

Power drill & bits

Waterproof wood glue

1⅝" deck screws

2 × 4" pine

3" deck screws

Tracing paper

Trim router & straight bit

Sandpaper

Putty knife

Wood putty

Exterior ebony wood stain

Paintbrush

Model paintbrush

Red oil-based model paint

3-5 lag screws

CUT LIST

(1) 1½ × 1½ × 11" pine entry baffle

(2) 1½ × 3½ × 24½" pine sides

(1) 1½ × 3½ × 11" pine spreader

(1) ½ × 14 × 24½" plywood back

(1) ½ × 14 × 19" plywood front

(1) ½ × 6½ × 14" plywood roof

1 Cut all the pieces to the dimensions listed on the cut list. Cut one end of each 2 × 4" side to a 10° angle. Bevel one end of the front, back, and roof to 10°. Rip down the baffle to 1½".

2 Measure and cut the fiberglass screen for the inside faces of the front and back. The screen should run down the center of the front and back, with a 1½" margin on each side (it should stop 1½" from what will be the bottom of the front and the same distance from what will be the top of the back). Staple the screen panels in place [**fig. A**].

C

3 Align the top angle of one side with the beveled end of the back, and glue and screw the back to the edge of the side with 1⅝" deck screws. Repeat with the opposite side.

4 Position the 2 × 4 spreader on edge between the two sides. Place it as close as possible to the top, but ensure that it won't interfere with the roof placement. Screw the spreader in position through the sides using 3" deck screws [**fig. B**].

5 Enlarge the bat line design and transfer it to tracing paper (see diagram on page 156). Use the tracing paper to transfer the design to the outside face of the front (oriented with the top of the bat to the beveled end side). Use a trim router with a straight bit to carve the design. Sand to clean up as necessary [**fig. C**]. (As an alternative, you can simply paint the bat line figure on the front freehand, after you've painted the front black.)

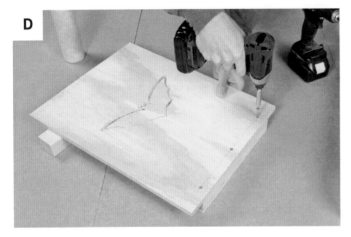

D

6 Fasten the entry baffle at the bottom end of the front board (opposite the beveled end and on the face opposite the bat design). The baffle should be positioned flush with the bottom edge and centered so that there is a 1½" border on either side. Glue and screw the baffle in place with 1⅝" deck screws [**fig. D**].

7 Align the top of the front with the angled cuts on each side. Glue and screw the front to the sides with 1⅝" deck screws.

8 Place the roof on top of the box with the back (beveled) edge flush with the back. Glue and screw the roof in place with 1⅝" deck screws [**fig. E**].

E

9 Putty over the screw heads and sand the box all over. Stain the box — except for the inside but including the exposed face of the back — with ebony stain. Use oil-based red paint and a fine brush to paint inside the lines of the bat design on the front. Mount the box to an existing structure with three to five lag screws driven through the exposed lower portion of the back.

CHICKADEE SLAT HOUSE

This elegant and sophisticated birdhouse is actually surprisingly simple to construct. The body is made of cedar slats that overlap in an alternating pattern. The construction creates a unique appearance thanks to the ends of the longer slats being stained darker than the face of the slats. That pleasing contrast—and the simple, linear nature of the design—gives the birdhouse a distinctly mid-century modern vibe. But you can certainly play with the look to suit your own tastes. For instance, the house would really grab some attention with alternating slats painted in different primary colors.

This particular design was developed for the black-capped chickadee, but you can easily modify it for other songbirds. In most cases, the change would require nothing more than a different size entry hole.

However, you'll find it's well worth sticking with the intended occupant because all of the seven species of chickadees are wonderful backyard companions. Featuring a distinctive black-and-white head over a plump body, the black-capped chickadee is the most common, with a presence in every northern state in the United States. These gregarious birds aren't timid about meeting their human hosts face to face. The bird is active all through the day, providing endless amusement to bird watchers.

Chickadees eat a diverse diet, including garden pests such as caterpillars and larvae. However, they also will feast on beneficial invertebrates, such as spiders. They eat seeds of all kinds and berries from a range of plants. They will gladly eat from feeders, whether it's a traditional seed-filled platform feeder or a peanut butter–slathered suet feeder. They also have an entertaining habit of caching food, and chickadees boast an impressive memory for where they've hidden snacks.

Chickadees are incredibly comfortable around humans and will even use their hosts as feeders!

Don't be fooled by how bold chickadees can be around humans; they are subject to attack by a number of different predators. Pick a location for the box that is removed from other trees or overhanging thick branches that could be used by squirrels or raccoons to get to the birdhouse.

Wrens are a particular threat. If you have house wrens in your area, it's a good idea to add a wren guard to the birdhouse as soon as chickadees set up residence there. (A wren guard is basically a thin wood shield positioned about 2" in front of the entry hole, blocking line of sight to the hole. The chickadees will already know where the hole is, and wrens won't detect the hole and identify the birdhouse as a possible nesting site.)

SLAT HOUSE MAINTENANCE

It's best not to disturb the slat birdhouse until you're sure the eggs have been laid because chickadees will abandon a nest site if their nest is disturbed before brooding. Chickadees will lay six to eight tiny eggs. The adults will incubate the eggs for ten days to two weeks before they hatch. When checking the box, whistle or otherwise alert the adults that you are there, so as not to panic the birds. Although chickadees are very comfortable in close contact with humans, when they feel threatened they will do what's known as a snake display, a distinctive show of hissing and feinting an attack at the threat. The eggs will be covered with what's known as a fur plug, so they might not be visible. Be very careful in checking the nest. You can lightly pull up the plug to check on the eggs, but do not touch them because chickadee eggs are exceedingly fragile. Check for any problems and then close up the house.

HOW TO BUILD A
CHICKADEE SLAT HOUSE

TOOLS & MATERIALS

Tape measure

1 × 4" cedar

1 × 1" cedar

¾" high-quality exterior-grade plywood

Table or circular saw

Carpenter's pencil

Straight edge

Speed square

Power drill & bits

Exterior semi-transparent deck stain

Rag

Metal straightedge

2 × 4" pine

Waterproof wood glue

Bar clamps

1⅛" Forstner bit

Utility knife or rotary tool

4D 1½" galvanized finish nails

2" butt hinge

Black plastic push-to-close cabinet catch

2" deck screws

Putty knife

Wood putty

Sandpaper

Paintbrush (for touch ups)

6 × 6 × 6" to 10" post

CUT LIST

[10] ¾ × 3½ × 4" cedar short slats

[10] ¾ × 3½ × 5½" cedar long slats

[1] ¾ × 8½ × 8½" plywood roof

[1] ¾ × 4 × 4" plywood floor

[1] 1½ × 3½ × 24" pine post mount

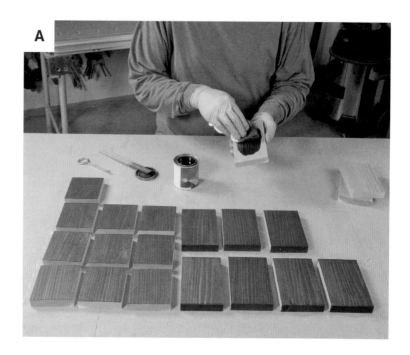

A

1 Cut all the pieces to the dimensions listed on the cut list. Drill ¼" holes in a cross pattern on the floor. Cut one end of the post-mount 2 × 4 to a point.

2 Use a rag to stain all the slats and the ends of just the long slats. Stain the post mount and roof [**fig. A**].

3 Once all the surfaces are dry, build one wall at a time, starting with the front. Working on a flat, level work surface that is covered with a clean drop cloth or cardboard, lay the slats out in a column to make the front. The surface is built with alternating short and long slats, starting with a short slat at the top. Lay the slats finished-side down. Measure and make registration marks for the position of the long slats (they should be centered side to side on the short slats with equal overhang on each side). Remove the slats, lay a light bead of wood glue on all inside edges, and reposition the slats, clamping them together until the glue dries [**fig. B**].

Note: You can make this process easier and more exact by clamping a long metal ruler or straightedge to the work surface. Use this as an alignment reference to make sure the panels end up flush along the long slat edges.

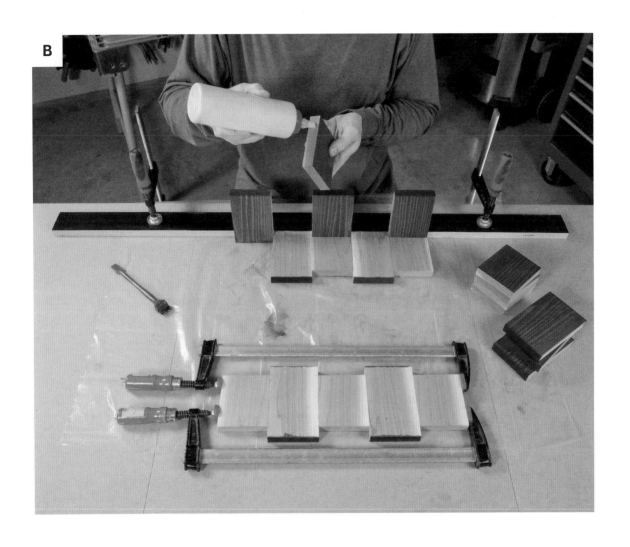

4 Mark the center of the entry hole 5¼" down from the top of the front and centered side to side. Use a Forstner bit to drill a 1⅛" hole centered on the mark [**fig. C**]. Mark lines side to side on the inside surface of the front every ½" from the bottom up to just below the hole. Score the lines with a utility knife or rotary tool [**fig. D**].

5 Nail the sides to the front and back with 4d 1½" galvanized finish nails. Nail the completed walls to the floor in the same way.

6 Drill three ¼" ventilation holes at the top of each side wall, spacing the holes equidistant along the width of the wall and about ¾" down from the top.

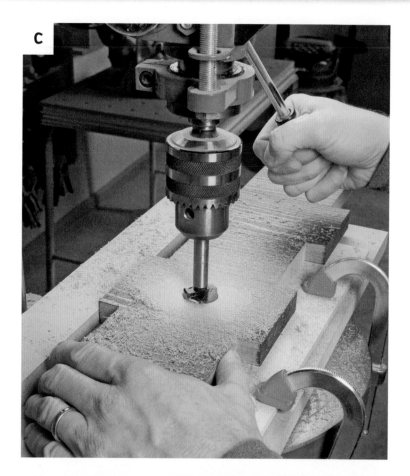

7 Set the roof in place and make key marks once you've verified that the overhang is equal all around. Mark the placement for the hinge on one side and the spring latch on the other. Remove the roof, drill pilot holes, and screw the hinge and latch catch to the roof using the supplied screws [**fig. E**].

8 Drill pilot holes and screw the catch body to the side wall. Replace the roof, and screw the hinge to the opposite side wall.

9 Position the post-mount 2 × 4 with the top edge butted to the underside of the roof and with the post centered side to side on the back. Drill pilot holes and screw the post mount to the back with 2" deck screws [**fig. F**].

10 For a finished look, dab wood putty over any exposed nail heads, sand smooth, and touch up with the stain. Mount the birdhouse to a sturdy 6 × 6" post with the bottom of the birdhouse 6 to 10" above the ground.

E

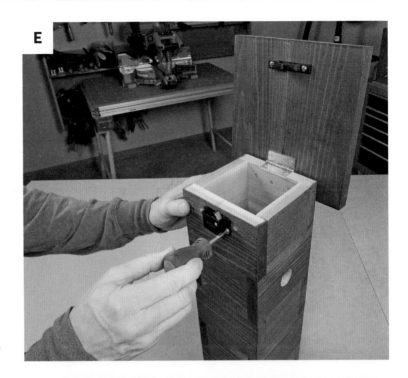

F

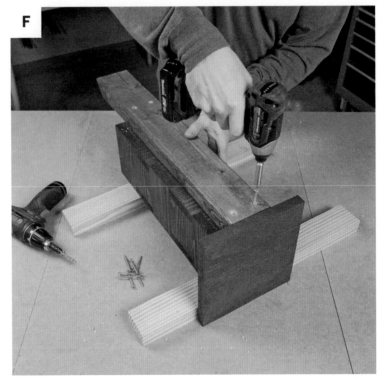

A NUTHATCH WEDGE

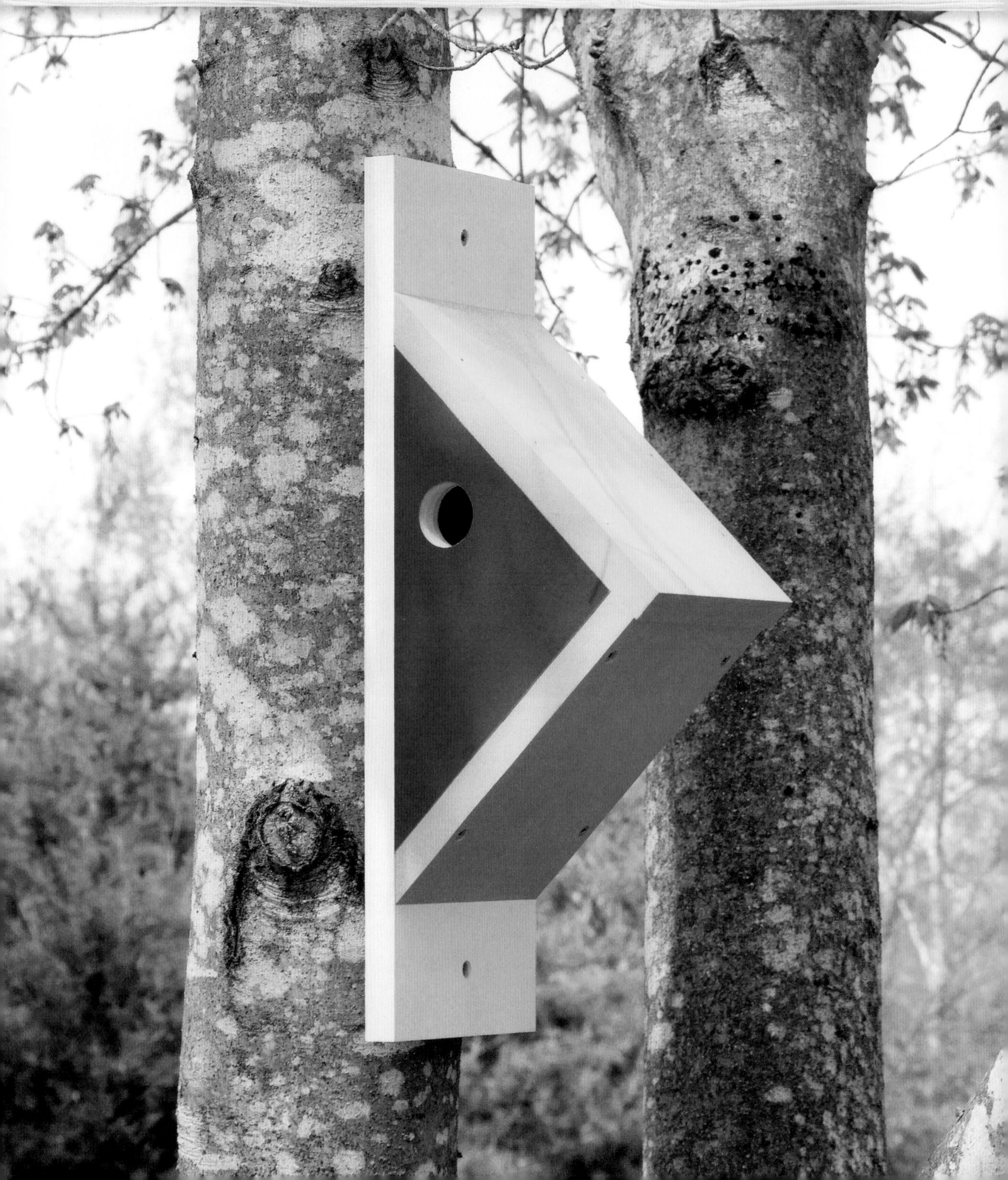

The nuthatch is a subtly colored bird but a beautiful and musical pleasure to have as a backyard resident.

Looking like a slice of pie, this distinctive birdhouse offers an unusual shape for the garden and an attractive nesting box. The shape is accented by a bold color scheme. This design is finished with a Scandinavian flag blue-and-yellow combination, but you can switch it up with your favorite colors (just stay away from bold reds).

This style of birdhouse is actually appropriate for a number of different songbirds, but this particular design is intended for the wide-ranging white-breasted nuthatch. This bird is a bit of an oddity among small songbirds; it has unusual habits and a loud song that make it worth inviting into the backyard.

The birds will often forage upside down on tree trunks, hunting insects in cracks in the bark. Seeing the birds busy looking for food with their tail feathers to the sky can be amusing. They will also jam nuts and seeds into bark cracks and use their pointed bills to crack the hulls or shells open, almost like the action of woodpecker.

Nuthatches prefer old-growth trees, and you're more likely to draw them to your yard if you have several. You can also make your backyard more appealing with a suet or birdseed feeder. They are especially fond of sunflower seeds and peanuts or peanut butter–smeared suet. Nuthatches are social birds who have little fear of humans; they are not above eating their favorite seeds right out of the landlord's hand.

If you happen to attract overwintering birds, you may be treated to a large mixed flock of songbirds in the colder months. Nuthatches often forage in the winter with titmice and chickadees. The large numbers and diversity in the group make it easier to find food and detect potential predators. Although you won't have to do a lot in terms of birdhouse maintenance, you can help keep your charges safe by using one or more predator guards on the wedge birdhouse.

TOOLS & MATERIALS

Tape measure

Carpenter's pencil

Speed square

Table or circular saw

2 × 6" pine

¾" exterior-grade plywood

1 × 6" cedar board

Power drill & bits

1¼" Forstner bit

Palm sander

80-grit sanding sheets

Paintbrush

Exterior wood primer

Exterior Persian blue paint

Exterior bright white paint

Exterior Philippine yellow paint

Painter's tape

Silicone adhesive

2" deck screws

1½" galvanized finish nails

(4) 1" stainless-steel screws

Putty knife

Wood putty

CUT LIST

(1) ¾ × 5 × 18" pine back

(1) ¾ × 5½ × 9" cedar roof

(1) ¾ × 6 × 8¼" cedar floor

(2) ¾ × 7¼ × 10¼" plywood sides

HOW TO BUILD A
NUTHATCH WEDGE

A

B

1 Cut all the pieces to the dimensions listed on the cut list. Cut the two sides from a 7¼" square of exterior grade plywood. Use a speed square to mark a diagonal line corner to corner [**fig. A**] and then cut along the line with a circular saw.

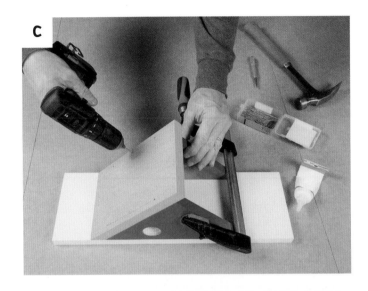

C

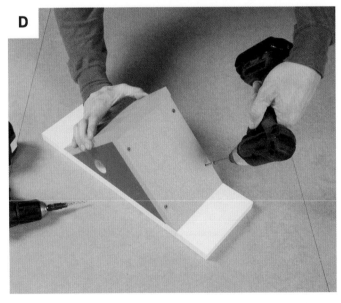

D

2 Measure and mark the entry hole 3" in from a base end and 1" from the long base of one triangle. Drill the entry hole with a 1¼" Forstner bit. Drill three ¼" ventilation holes in the opposite side wall at a point where the base meets a short side on the opposite side wall.

3 Bevel one end of the roof and floor 45°. Measure and mark two parallel reference lines 10¼" apart and centered along the length of the back 2 × 6. Sand all the pieces with 80-grit sandpaper. Paint each section individually: paint the roof and floor yellow, the two sides blue, and the mounting post bright white [**fig. B**].

4 Use the reference line to position the sides, each with the long base contacting the back. Drill pilot holes and glue with silicone adhesive and screw the back to each side using 2" deck screws. (The outside faces are flush with the outside edges of the back.)

5 Check that the roof and bottom fit snuggly onto the sides and adjust as necessary. Set the roof in position and drill pilot holes down into the edges of the sides. Coat the edges with silicone adhesive and carefully nail the roof to the sides with 1½" galvanized finish nails [**fig. C**].

6 Set the floor into position. Drill two small holes in the joint of the roof and floor and one hole centered along the beveled bottom edge of the floor and into the back. Screw the floor into place with four 1" stainless-steel screws at the sides [**fig. D**]. (This allows for easy removal of the bottom when it comes time to clean the house.)

7 Touch up the paint as necessary to cover any nail or screw heads. Mount the birdhouse on a post or a solid fence, about 10" above the ground.

4

SPECIALTY SMALL BIRDHOUSES

MANY HOME CRAFTSPEOPLE WANT A UNIQUE LOOK if they're going to invest time and effort in building a birdhouse. If you fall into this category, the projects that follow will hold special appeal. The birdhouses in this chapter were all designed with a fashion-first approach. They are interesting, attention-grabbing alternatives to more traditional birdhouse designs. They are playful, whimsical, and just plain fun.

The beauty of these designs lies in their flexibility. There are many ways to personalize each of these creations to make them truly your own. The simplest option is, of course, to change the color scheme. But the potential variations are far more diverse. Use the techniques described for ornamentation on many of these projects to fashion different add-ons that more accurately reflect your own tastes.

However, it's wise to stick fairly close to the dimensions listed so that, no matter how beautiful and fun your birdhouse might be, it can still be used by songbirds looking for a temporary home. Lastly, keep in mind that these types of highly creative and whimsical projects are wonderful ways to get children interested in woodwork and birding at the same time (and get them away from the many electronic screens in their lives!).

A pair of nesting eastern bluebirds are ideal tenants for a PVC birdhouse.

PVC pipe may, at first glance, seem like an odd choice of material for a birdhouse, but it's actually ideal. PVC is incredibly durable, nontoxic, easy to fabricate, and well-suited to the dimensional needs of most small birds. As this project clearly shows, it can be finished in a number of ways that make the surface far more attractive than the dull white of plain PVC pipe.

The design for this structure is based on a well-established bluebird birdhouse style known as the Gilbertson design. For that reason, the entry hole and dimensions are meant to accommodate bluebirds, but it's exceedingly easy to adapt the birdhouse to other small songbird species. In any case, the decorative style is meant to be naturalistic, with a faux aspen bark appearance. The finish looks convincingly like an actual tree. As a bonus, the white exterior ensures that the interior of the birdhouse doesn't become overheated under even direct midday sun.

Although the interior is smaller than most other birdhouses, there is still enough space in a section of PVC 4" pipe for the birds to comfortably nest. Aggressive sparrows find the shape and appearance of the PVC house unappealing,

meaning that they will leave it for bluebird families. The material is also lightweight enough to easily hang from even flimsy tree branches (where squirrels are less likely to venture).

This particular birdhouse has been mounted to a roof with significant overhang to keep your feathered friends out of the elements. The body of the birdhouse is fixed to a PVC cap that serves as a floor. A dowel serves as a quick-release mechanism for easy floor removal and cleaning of the birdhouse in the off season. It's a good idea to dump out old nests and any other waste material far from the site of the birdhouse to avoid attracting predators. Fortunately, you'll find that PVC is also incredibly easy to clean.

Although the house in this project is meant to be hung from a tree branch, the standard Gilbertson design was developed to be mounted on a predator-deterring ½" electrical conduit post. If you prefer to use this method (a good idea if your yard hosts many potential predators), you can replicate the mounting part of a Gilbertson house by drilling a ½" hole in a 2 × 2 cleat and screwing the cleat along the back edge of the roof's underside. You could also substitute rebar or other post material.

TOOLS & MATERIALS

Tape measure

Marker

Miter saw or handsaw

1 × 8" cedar

4" dia. Schedule 40 PVC pipe

Workbench clamp

Awl or center punch

1½" hole saw

Sandpaper

Utility knife (optional)

¾" plywood

Jigsaw

Power drill & bits

Straightedge

4" dia. Schedule 40 PVC cap

½" dowel

1" stainless-steel wood screws

1" paintbrush

Exterior dark gray paint

Exterior gloss white paint

Silicone sealant

(2) 1⅝" zinc-plated screw eyes

#12 zinc-plated chain

CUT LIST

(1) ¾ × 7 × 8" roof

(1) ¾ × 2 × 7½" cedar

(1) 4" dia. plywood ceiling

(1) 8" PVC pipe body

(1) ½ × 5" dowel

HOW TO BUILD A
SONGBIRD PVC APARTMENT

1 Cut the pieces for the project to the dimensions on the cut list. To cut the pipe for the body of the birdhouse, use a miter saw and make repeated cuts by rotating the pipe. You can also use a jigsaw or handsaw with the pipe held in a homemade X cradle.

2 Clamp the cut pipe. Measure and mark the center of the entry hole 5" from one end. Tap a guide point at the mark with an awl or center punch. Drill out the hole with a 1½" hole saw (or use the appropriate size hole saw for the small cavity nester you're hoping to attract) [**fig. A**].

3 Use sandpaper or a utility knife to remove any burrs from the cut edges and to smooth the entry hole edges.

4 Use one end of the PVC birdhouse body as a template to trace a circle on a large square of exterior grade ¾" plywood. Use a jigsaw to cut out the circle, working inside the traced line. Check that the disc fits into the end of the PVC body and sand down any areas that prevent it from sliding into the end. Drill a triangle pattern of ¼" drainage holes centered on the PVC cap, which will serve as the floor of the birdhouse.

5 Use a straightedge to mark opposite sides of the PVC cap for the dowel holes (the holes should be centered top to bottom on the edge of the cap). With the PVC body in a vise or clamped to a work surface, slide the cap onto the top of the body and drill two opposing ½" holes. Check that the ½" locking dowel will pass through each hole (the fit should be snug) [**fig. B**].

C

D

E

6 Slip the body over the ceiling disc and drill four pilot holes at cardinal points around the bottom of the body. Drill pilot holes for the mounting screws [**fig. C**].

7 Sand the PVC pipe body and floor all around to remove any markings and dull the sheen of the pipe. Sit the body upside down, with the floor in place, on a homemade turntable [a round plywood base with a 3" screw sticking up out of it will work; mount the ceiling of the bird house on the screw]. Use a flat, extremely dark gray [almost black] paint [automotive primer is a good alternative]. Wet the paintbrush and then dab it almost dry. Slowly rotate the PVC body, holding the brush in place so the edge bristles graze the surface, laying down an inconsistent horizontal line [**fig. D**]. Repeat, moving down the body. When you're satisfied with the look of the lines, wet the brush and dab and smush to create a few irregular circular blemishes randomly up and down the body. Let the paint dry.

8 Screw the ¾ × 2 × 7" piece to the back edge of the roof. Paint the roof and removable dowel semi-gloss white.

9 Screw the ceiling to the roof of the birdhouse [**fig. E**]. Attach the cap to the bottom of the birdhouse with the removable dowel.

10 Drill two pilot holes in the top of the roof centered side to side and in about 2" from each. Dab silicone sealant into the holes and screw in two 1⅝" zinc-plated screw eyes.

11 Hang the birdhouse with #12 chain. Run from one screw eye over a tree branch or other overhang and down to the other screw eye. Hang the birdhouse so that the entry hole is 5" above ground level [or the correct height for the species you're hoping to attract]. Position the house out of the wind and direct sun, with a clear line of site all around.

WREN COTTAGE

Bewick's wren

Carolina wren

House wren

I f you've ever dreamed of a pretty little back-yard guest house that would delight visitors—something adorably cute and comfy—look no further. This birdhouse makes a truly lovely garden decoration with its wonderfully unique shape and gingerbread detailing. Don't be surprised if you fall in love with the design and feel the need to build a human-sized version for your in-laws and out-of-town friends.

The birdhouse, though, attracts just one type of visitor, and it's a charming—if rather drab—songbird. Wrens produce bursts of song that are sure to make you happy, and even though they look like feathered accountants, these are the circus clowns of birds. Their frenetic activity and funny behavior is sure to amuse any backyard bird watchers.

There are actually three wren species that blanket the United States with their respective ranges. The Bewick wren is found along the West Coast and throughout the Southwest; the Carolina wren spreads throughout the Eastern United States and the Southeast; and the house wren is found throughout the United States except for small sections of the southernmost border. Depending on the species, the birds brood from late March through the end of summer. All wrens are extremely territorial and prefer a half-acre to call their own.

Wrens are welcome lodgers because they vacuum up undesirable garden insects, including boll weevils, stink bugs, leafhoppers, snails, and sow bugs. However, they do like fruit, so you'll need to take steps to protect any cherry trees or fruit bushes you have in your yard—unless you're willing to share the harvest.

Wrens, especially house wrens, are unusually aggressive. They will chase other small birds out of the area, to take over a nest. The odd part is, the male house wren will work hard to create several nests before the female settles in. For all their activity and energy, the birds don't require a lot of living space. This modest classic hexagonal design provides all the room a wren couple needs to raise a family and stay safe and secure.

This house is constructed of ¾" cedar, which provides a long-lasting construction largely impervious to the elements and insect infestation. Although the fine details of this house beg for complementary paint colors, if you decide to simplify the structure and leave the house natural, it will weather to a handsome light gray.

HOW TO BUILD A
WREN COTTAGE

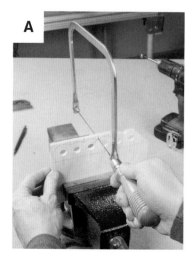

A

B

TOOLS & MATERIALS

Tape measure

Speed square

Carpenter's pencil

Table saw

1 × 10" cedar board

Miter saw

Power drill & bits

1⅛" Forstner bit

(2) ¼" balsa wood pieces

French curve or other template for scallop trim

Utility knife or coping saw

Bar clamps

Waterproof wood glue

6d 1½" nails

(1) 2" zinc-plated gate hook eye latch

(1) 1½" zinc-plated butt hinges

Masking or painter's tape

Paintbrushes

Exterior flat lavender paint

Exterior gloss white paint

Putty knife

Wood putty

Sandpaper

Silicone sealant

(4) 1" screw eyes

4" #16 jack chain

CUT LIST

(2) ¾ × 8 × 8⅞" front & back

(1) ¾ × 2½ × 5½" floor

(2) ¾ × 5⁹⁄₁₆ × 5½" sides

(1) ¾ × 7¾ × 8" long roof

(1) ¾ × 7 × 8" long roof

(2) ¼ × 1 × 7" balsa wood gingerbread

(1) ⅛ × ¼ × 2¼" balsa wood lintel

(2) ⅛ × ¼ × 4⅛" balsa wood door trim

1 Cut all the pieces to rough size according the dimensions on the cut list. Make the angle cuts on the front following the diagram on page 59 and then use the front as a template to mark the cuts for the back. Measure and mark the entry hole 5" up from the bottom of the front and centered side to side, and drill it with a 1⅛" Forstner bit.

2 Carefully measure and mark the scallop trim on one ¼" balsa wood piece using a French curve or other template (see diagram on page 59). Measure and mark for ⅜" holes centered edge to edge and centered in the width of each scallop. Cut out the scallop pattern with a utility knife or coping saw [**fig. A**]. Drill the holes and then use the piece to transfer the gingerbread details to the second ¼" balsa wood blank. Finally, cut one end of each piece to a 45° angle.

3 Carefully bevel the top of each side (67½°) and the two long edges of the floor (22½°) [**fig. B**].

Note: *As a shortcut and to ensure a flush fit, use the front to mark the ends of the floor for the bevel cut and the bottom edges of the roof sections for their bevel cuts.*

Drill three ¼" vent holes in a triangle at the peak of the front and back sections. Drill a triangle of ventilation holes in the floor. Cut the ends of the balsa wood lintel to a 10° angle.

4 Check that all the pieces fit as they should against the edge bevels. Clamp the floor to a work surface with the narrower face down. Fasten the front to one long end of the floor by drilling pilot holes and then gluing and nailing the front in place with 6d 1½" nails. Attach the back to the opposite floor edge in the same way. In both cases, make sure the roughest side of the wood faces in.

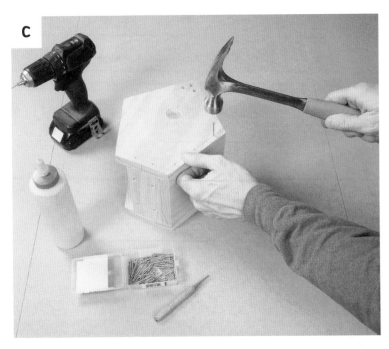

5 Position one side wall between the front and back and drill three pilot holes along each edge to attach the front and back to the wall. Glue and nail the wall in place [**fig. C**].

6 Attach the narrower roof section on the side of the birdhouse with the wall attached. Make sure the roof is flush with the peak of the front and rear walls and flush at the back with the back of the rear wall. Drill pilot holes and glue and nail the roof in place to the front and back walls [**fig. D**].

7 Repeat the process with the wider roof section, which should overlap the first roof section at the peak. Drill pilot holes and glue and nail the section along the joint, as well as to the front and back walls.

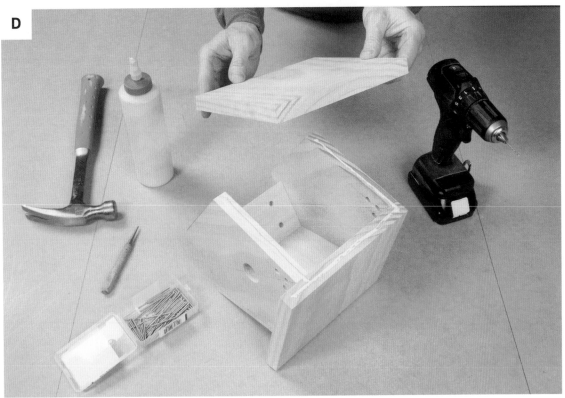

8 Putty over nail heads and sand them smooth as desired. Paint the birdhouse, but mask off a strip of bare wood to which you'll attach the gingerbread trim. Paint the birdhouse the lavender color shown (being careful not to get any paint inside the structure). Sand and paint the balsa wood pieces bright gloss white.

9 Place the second side wall and mark the screw holes for the hinge that will connect the wall to the roof. The hinge should be centered front to back. Remove the wall and attach the hinge to it. Then, reposition the wall and screw the hinge to the roof using the supplied screws [**fig. E**].

10 Fasten the 2" gate hook eye latch to the underside of the floor and the bottom edge of the hinged wall, so that when the hook is latched, the side wall will be held tightly closed.

11 Glue and clamp the gingerbread trim in place to the front wall, along the eave of the roof, so that both pieces meet at the angle end cuts. Measure and mark for the placement of the door pieces. Fasten them in place with silicone sealant. Mark a faux window and doorknob, and paint the window light gray and the doorknob gold or black [**fig. F**].

12 Fasten the birdhouse to a tree or post or use screw eyes and chain to hang the birdhouse from a sturdy tree branch.

E

F
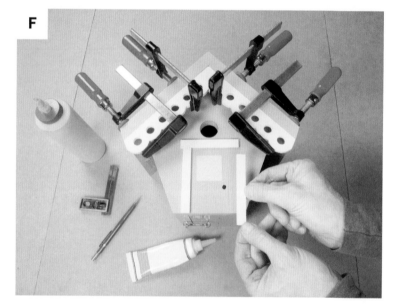

CUT DIAGRAMS FOR WREN COTTAGE

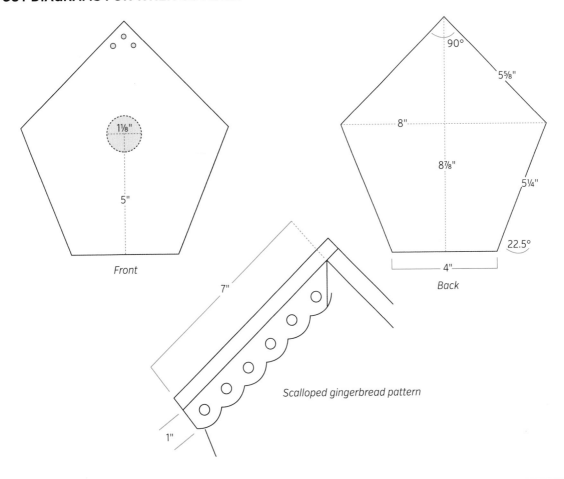

Front

Back

Scalloped gingerbread pattern

THE RIGHT SITE

Wrens are sensitive to the cold, so the birdhouse entrance should be positioned out of the wind. For the same reason, the house should ideally receive early morning sunlight and be shaded in the afternoon. House wrens don't mind a hanging birdhouse that swings a little, but if you're attracting other species of wren, you'll need to fix the box to a post, fence, or tree. Wrens are comfortable with human activity, so the birdhouse can be relatively close to a house, shed, or patio. Be aware that even if a nest appears in the birdhouse you've put up, the wrens may ultimately decide to nest elsewhere. That's why some backyard birders looking to attract wrens put up more than one house to guarantee success. Don't let the hinged side wall on this house fool you; wrens do not like their nests disturbed, so you won't have to check the birdhouse during the breeding season.

MOD SQUAD PAD

The eastern phoebe is on of several songbirds who would be happy to call this hip pad home.

Looks matter. Although a birdhouse is all about practicality from the bird's perspective, it is any homeowner's opportunity to show off a sense of flair and design and create a strong decorative element in the yard or garden. This birdhouse takes that principle a few steps beyond simply painting a birdhouse in colors to actually designing one that looks like a mid-century modern home.

Although it's intended for bluebirds, the Mod Squad Pad can easily be adapted for any small songbird, from the house wren to the eastern phoebe. Subtle changes to the floor plan or dimensions won't radically affect the look of the house. You can also play with the color scheme; the orange and blue used on the house as designed are just accents. More coverage, or different colors, would make the house stand out even more.

You can also embellish the basic design here with more mid-century modern touches. For instance, a small piece of decorative perforated metal sheet cut to fit between the roof and floor at the front of the house, and painted simple bright white, could bring a period splash to the look. Texturing one or more surfaces to look like poured concrete could do the same.

Because this is a decorative birdhouse, consider mounting it on a decorative post—even if you simply paint a 6 × 6" post. The format of the birdhouse makes it ungainly to mount in a tree, and it would look a little unusual hung from a branch or an overhang, although that is an option. You can post mount the birdhouse by creating a homemade flange of 2 × 2" cleats screwed to the bottom around the perimeter of a square matching the post's dimensions. Screw the flanges to the post to secure the birdhouse.

TOOLS & MATERIALS

Tape measure

Carpenter's pencil

½" birch plywood

Circular or table saw

Power drill & bits

1⅜" Forstner bit

Waterproof wood glue

Bar clamps

4d 1½" galvanized finish nails

Speed square

2" stainless-steel butt hinge

2" stainless-steel hook-&-eye latch

2" deck screws

Putty knife

Wood putty

Palm sander

Sandpaper

Paintbrush

Exterior flat orange paint

Exterior flat blue paint

Exterior clear finish

CUT LIST

(2) ½ × 6 × 6½" back & front

(1) ½ × 7 × 12" roof

(2) ½ × 1 × 6½" decorative posts

(1) ½ × 7 × 10" floor

(2) ½ × 5 × 6½" sides

(1) ½ × 4 × 11" backer (optional)

HOW TO BUILD A
MOD SQUAD PAD

1 Mark the cuts for all the pieces on a sheet of plywood. Lay out the cut lines so that you minimize the actual number of cuts you'll need to make. Measure twice to ensure all the pieces are the correct dimensions. Use a circular or table saw to cut out all the pieces.

2 Drill the front access hole offset of center. Measure and mark a starting point 5" in from one short edge and 4" in from one long edge of the front. Drill the hole with the correct size of Forstner bit for the bird you're hoping to attract (the 1⅜" hole shown here accommodates bluebirds) [**fig. A**].

3 Drill ¼" drainage holes at each corner of the floor 3" in from what will be the front, 1½" from the back, and 3" from the sides. Drill three ¼" ventilation holes centered along one short edge of each side.

4 Mark the positions of the back, side, and front walls on the floor. The side walls are 2" in from each end, and the front is 1" in from the front edge of the floor; the back will be flush to the back edge of the floor [**fig. B**].

5 Lay a bead of glue along one short edge of the back and clamp it to the floor as marked. Drill pilot holes and nail the pieces together with 4d 1½" galvanized finish nails.

6 Fasten each side wall in the same way, laying an additional bead of glue along the back edge of each side before setting it in place. Drill pilot holes and nail the back to the walls using three nails along each edge.

7 Assemble the front, back, and sides into a box by gluing and nailing the walls together. Clamp the construction down and nail the bottom to the walls [**fig. C**].

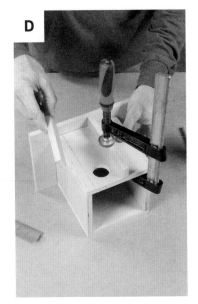

8 Use a speed square to draw plumb lines on the front, ½" on either side of the entry hole. Glue a post in place with the inside face of the post aligned with one plumb line. Glue the opposite post with the inside aligned with the opposite plumb line [**fig. D**].

9 Set the roof in place. Align one side edge with the floor and the front with the front of the floor. Make key marks for position of the roof on the walls. Position the hinge on the underside of the short roof overhang and the side wall and mark the location. Remove the roof and screw the hinge in place. Replace the roof and screw the hinge to the wall [**fig. E**]. Screw the hook and latch to the opposite side roof overhang and side.

10 If you're using the mounting/backer board, attach it now. Lay the birdhouse face down. Position the mounting board so that it will project above the top of the birdhouse. Center the board between the side walls and with the bottom flush with the bottom edge of the birdhouse. Drill pilot holes for the mounting board and then glue and screw it in place with 2" deck screws [**fig. F**].

11 Putty over all the screw and nail heads and lightly sand the house all over. Paint the front edges of the posts blue. Paint the area between the two posts orange (being careful not to get any paint on the inside edges of the hole). Finish the rest of the house natural with a clear exterior finish (or paint it in your own color scheme). Mount the house on a post by screwing through the top of the mounting board at a height that is appropriate for the species you're looking to attract (about 5" for bluebirds).

The Acadian flycatcher is just one of many flycatcher species, most of which will gladly take up residence in a custom backyard motel.

Sometimes what you need is a bold yet contemporary accent for your landscape. If you're willing to go a little edgy, this bird lodging will be an unmistakably distinctive visual. A riff on the budget traveler's crash pad of choice, this cinderblock birdhouse brings rough-hewn texture and visual weight to a structure usually defined by smooth surfaces and light—bordering on fragile—construction.

This particular project is intended for flycatchers, a group of eleven species of songbirds found around the country. As the name indicates, these birds are insectivores. They perch on tree twigs and wait for insects to fly within sight, and then they pluck their prey out of midair. They will also feast on caterpillars and spiders, given half a chance.

All flycatchers have interesting markings, but they are not generally a very colorful type. They do make themselves known, however, with a distinctive, repetitive chirping call. If you're looking to attract flycatchers to your yard, it's wise to check with the local agricultural extension office or Audubon chapter for information on the species most common in your area.

Of course, the space afforded by the cavity in the cinderblock is perfectly suitable to a number of small songbirds. All you have to do is change the diameter of the entry hole. Want to put your own stamp on the look of the project? Although we've left it natural, you shouldn't hesitate to paint the cinderblock (a bright yellow would work perfectly with the bright white wood front). Just make sure to use concrete patio paint for the best results.

TOOLS & MATERIALS

Tape measure
8" half cinderblock
Carpenter's pencil
1 × 6" pine board
Jigsaw
Power drill & bits
½" masonry bit
Sandpaper
⅜" eyebolt, flat washers, & hex nut
⅞" box wrench
1¾" Forstner bit
1½" wood screws
Putty knife
Wood putty
Paintbrush
Exterior primer
Exterior gloss white paint
1" pipe strap
4" #16 jack chain

CUT LIST

(2) ¾ × 5⅛ × 5⅛" front & back
(2) ¾ × 2 × 6⅛" connectors

HOW TO BUILD A
FLYCATCHER CINDERBLOCK MOTEL

A

B

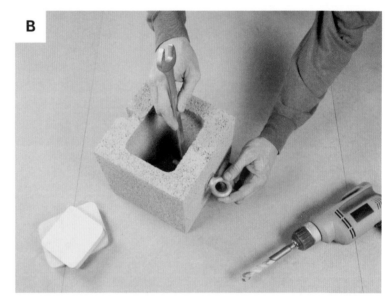

1 To mark the front and the back for cutting, lay the half cinderblock face down on a 1 × 6" pine board. Working from inside the core of the cinderblock, trace the shape of the opening on the board. Cut out the front with a jigsaw, sand the edges smooth as necessary, and check the fit into the core of the cinderblock (the fit can be snug but does not need to be precise—any gaps will allow for air flow) [**fig. A**].

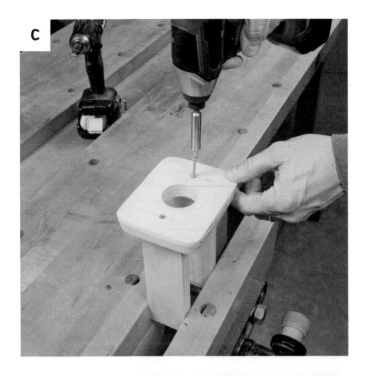

2 Use the back hole of the cinderblock as a template to mark the back for cutting (you may need to adjust; the openings are sometimes slightly different sizes). Cut the back out with a jigsaw, lightly sand, and check the fit. Cut the connectors from the same board.

3 Use a masonry bit to drill a ½" hole in the center of the top (opposite the grooved side) of the half cinderblock. Slip a round washer onto a ⅜" eyebolt, stick the eyebolt in the hole, and secure it with a second washer and hex nut. Tighten it snugly [**fig. B**].

4 Measure and mark the center of the entry hole centered top to bottom and side to side. Drill the hole using a 1¾" Forstner bit.

5 Center the end of one connecter lengthwise along one edge of the front. Drill a pilot hole, and fasten the front to the connector with a 1½" wood screw. Repeat with the opposite connector [**fig. C**].

6 Slide the front in place on one side of the core cavity. Slide the back in the opposite side, butted against the free ends of the connectors. Adjust the connector lengths as necessary to ensure a snug fit for the back. Drill pilot holes through the back and into the connectors.

7 Remove the front and putty over the screw heads. When dry, sand the entire front and then prime and paint it an exterior gloss white.

Optional: If you're painting the cinderblock, prime and paint it with concrete paint at this time.

8 Replace the front. Screw a pipe strap to the back and screw the back to the connectors through the predrilled holes using 1½" wood screws [**fig. D**]. Hang the birdhouse from a very thick branch or very secure overhang using chain.

The purple martin is a large, impressive bird with dramatic, dark plumage.

The large complex structure in this project is unique among birdhouses because its intended occupants are fairly unique among birds. Purple martins roost in colonies. That means that any birdhouse meant for the species must accommodate far more than just a single brooding pair. This particular structure accommodates six couples, but if you're confident that there are purple martins in your neck of the woods on a regular basis, you might want to build more than one of these; some purple martin colonies number in the hundreds!

Despite their name, purple martins are actually a species of sparrow. Much larger than most sparrows, with a broad chest and an iridescent almost black coloring that is more solid on adult males, the martin will happily brood in the same neighborhood as other species of sparrow. As striking as their appearance is, the real fun in watching purple martins is seeing them hunt. They eat insects that they pluck—almost exclusively— right out of midair. This involves a lot of aerial acrobatics. Unfortunately, the birds hunt at a much higher altitude than most other birds, so if you want to watch them on the wing, you'll probably

need a good pair of binoculars. Surprisingly, purple martins not only eat on the wing, they drink in flight too. The birds will actually skim the surface of a body of water, scooping up a drink as they go.

The practice of hanging hollowed out gourds as a purple martin village began with Native American tribes and is still a tradition with many birders today. But a group of houses such as the one in this project is much more visually impressive.

This may look like an intimidating structure to build, but it's less challenging than you might think. Except for the angled roof cuts and bevels, the fabrication is fairly straightforward. There are a lot of fiddly pieces, but measure twice and cut once and you'll be fine. The entire birdhouse should take about a weekend to complete. You can customize the structure in a number of ways. If you are familiar with model making, it would be an easy chore to create balsa wood shutters for the entry holes, gingerbread trim on the roof, or even a widow's walk. You can also change up the color scheme to shades that more accurately reflect your tastes or even your own house's existing scheme.

TOOLS & MATERIALS

Tape measure

Carpenter's pencil

Straightedge

Circular or table saw

1 × 6" cedar board

¾" exterior grade plywood

⅝ × ⅝ × 48" self-stick plastic corner guard

⅛ × 1½ × 36" pine (ripped from 2 × 4)

¾ × ¾ × 36" square dowel (ripped from scrap stock)

Bar clamps

Power drill & bits

Jigsaw or router table/router with a ¾" bit & jig

(4) 2 × 2 × 5½" cleats

Sawhorses

2⅛" Forstner bit

Waterproof wood glue

2" deck screws

1½" deck screws

Construction adhesive

Hammer

Finish brads

Heat gun or hair dryer

Silicone sealant

Masking tape or duct tape

Paintbrush

Exterior primer

Exterior gloss black paint

continued on page 72

HOW TO BUILD A
PURPLE MARTIN COMPLEX

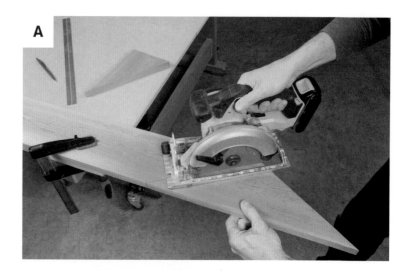

A

B

1 Cut all the pieces for the birdhouse to the dimensions on the cut list. Measure and mark an isosceles triangle on the face of one gable board. The triangle will have an 18" base with two 10" sides and a 118° top angle. The point of the triangle should be just short of the edge opposite the base. Cut the gable shape out using a circular saw. Use this gable as a template to mark and cut the second one [**fig. A**].

2 Clamp one gable on top of the other over a scrap piece. Measure and mark a triangle of ¼" ventilation holes at the peak of the gables, and drill the holes down through both gables [**fig. B**]. Bevel one long edge of each roof panel to a 59° angle.

3 Cut the ¾" edge slots for the dividers [**fig. C**]. These must be done precisely, whatever method you choose. Start by carefully marking the slots. On the short dividers, the slots are positioned exactly in the center of the divider, with the outside edges of the slots 6" in from either edge. The slots for the long divider are positioned 6" in from each edge with the inside slot edges 6" from each other. All the slots should be 2¾" deep. The easiest way to cut them is with a jigsaw guided by clamped scrap used as a straight-edge. Alternatively, you can cut the slots on a router table with a ¾" bit or using a router with a ¾" bit and a jig.

4 Mark the entry holes on one side board. The 2⅛" holes are positioned with their bottoms 2" in from one long edge and positioned 3", 9¾", and 16½" from one end [**fig. D**].

*Optional: Measure and mark the exact center of the floor and draw a 5½" square around the center mark. Screw two cleats along opposite sides of the square, overlapping two more cleats, to create a mounting flange for post mounting [**fig. E**]. This will allow you to secure the floor of the complex to a 6 × 6" wood post.*

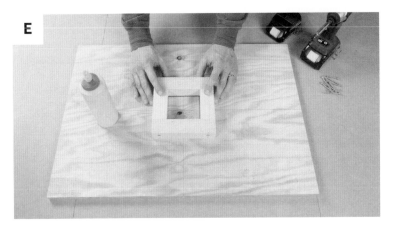

5 Clamp the marked side board on top of the second side board over a scrap piece or across sawhorses. Drill the entry holes with a 2⅛" Forstner bit.

TOOLS & MATERIALS

continued from page 70

(2) 2½" stainless-steel gate
hook-and-eye latches

Putty knife

Wood putty

Sandpaper

Exterior primer

Exterior gloss white paint

Exterior gloss yellow paint

CUT LIST

(2) ¾ × 5½ × 18" cedar gables

(2) ¾ × 5½ × 14¼" cedar ends

(2) ¾ × 5½ × 19½" cedar sides

(2) ¾ × 5½ × 12¾"cedar short dividers

(1) ¾ × 5½ × 19½" cedar long divider

(2) ¾ × 14¼ × 23½" plywood floor
and roof base

(2) ¾ × 11⅛ × 27" plywood roof

(26) ⅛ × 1½ × 28" pine shingles

(1) ⅝ × ⅝ × 27" plastic peak cap

(4) ½ × ½ × 5½" scrap wood columns

F

G

6 Attach one end board to one side board. Drill pilot holes and glue and screw the joint together with 2" deck screws. Fasten the opposite side to the opposite end of the end board in the same manner. Screw the opposite end to the opposite ends of the sides, creating the box frame for the birdhouse.

7 Position the frame on top of the floor, centered both ways. Make registration marks on the frame and floor. Dry fit the dividers in place and mark for a triangle of ¼" holes in the center of each compartment (for the center compartments, drill ventilation holes in a straight line to avoid the post-mount cleats on the underside of the floor). Remove the frame and dividers. Repeat the process with the roof base, marking the ventilation holes and key marks. Add those marks to both faces of the roof base [**fig. F**].

8 Clamp the floor on top of the roof over a scrap piece or on sawhorses (center the floor over the roof). Drill the drainage holes you marked on the floor all the way through the roof.

9 Set the frame upside down on a flat, level work surface (keeping in mind that the entry holes are closer to the top than the bottom of the frame). Set the floor on top of the frame so that the key marks are aligned with the frame and drill pilot holes every 2 to 3" around the frame. Screw the floor to the frame with 2" deck screws [**fig. G**].

10 Flip the frame right-side up. Set the dividers in place inside the frame with the long divider slotted into the short dividers [**fig. H**]. Ensure that the dividers form right angles with the frame, and then drill pilot holes and screw the frame to the divider ends with 2" deck screws.

11 Use the frame key marks on one side of the roof base to align the gables at either end of the roof base. Drill pilot holes and glue and screw the roof base to the gables with 1½" deck screws.

12 Position a roof panel on top of the gables so that there is an even overhang on the front and back and the beveled edge is at the peak of the roof. Drill pilot holes every 2" down into the gable edges and glue and screw the roof panel to the gables.

13 Position the second roof panel butted to the first at the peak and aligned front and back. Drill pilot holes as with the first roof panel and glue and screw the roof panel to the first roof panel and the top edges of the gables [**fig. I**].

14 Rip ⅛" strips off the edge of a clear pine 2 × 8 for all of the shingles. Mark the roof deck 1⅜" up from the bottom edges to set the first course and then ¾" up the roof from there; this creates a ⅛" drip edge along the bottom.

15 Fasten each course with a bead of construction adhesive applied just below the next layout line and along the top edge of the preceding shingle [**fig. J**]. Tack the shingles along their top edges with brads.

Note: Although you can buy balsa wood strips for this, it's easy and far less expensive to rip them from a scrap 2 × 4.

16 Use a heat gun or hair dryer on its hottest setting to soften the peak cap and press it into place to conform to the angle of the peak. Once cool, glue the peak cap in place along the roof peak using silicone sealant, so that the cap is flush on the roof on both edges. Tape it in place until it dries [**fig. K**]. Prime the roof with a quality exterior primer and then paint the entire roof, including the edges, black.

17 Place the roof structure on top of the compartments and check that the registration marks on the underside of the roof base are lined up with the frame (the roof base and floor should be aligned all around). Mark the positions for the three hinges on one frame side and the underside of the roof base and for the eye-and-hook latch screw eyes on the opposite side. (The hinges should be centered over the compartment divider ends.)

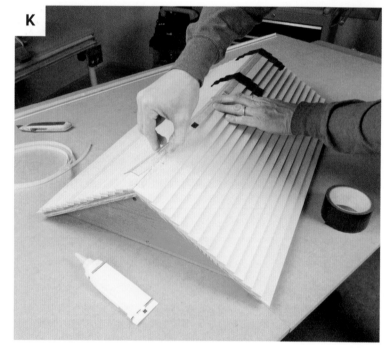

18 Remove the roof structure and screw the hinges and latch to the underside of the roof base. Replace the roof structure on top of the compartments—again making sure it is properly aligned—and screw the hinges to one end of the wall and the hook to the opposite wall where marked [**fig. L**].

19 Unscrew the roof hinge leaf, unhook the roof, and remove it. Paint the underside of the roof white, and the body and base yellow. Prime and paint the square dowel columns gloss white.

20 Carefully glue the basswood columns into each corner of the base. Drill very small pilot holes up from under the base into the columns. Screw the base to the columns with 2" exterior trim head screws [**fig. M**]. Replace the roof, screwing the hinge leaf back in place and hooking the opposite securely. Mount the house on a 6 × 6" post at least 10' from the ground.

L

M

The tufted titmouse is a low-key songbird but an attractive addition to any yard.

The rustic charm of this miniature log cabin is simply undeniable. Like its full-size cousin, this cabin features a construction of interlocked logs (in reality, ripped pieces of 2 × 4). There's even a log front porch. Best of all, although the design has lots of small parts, the actual construction doesn't require specialized skills and is forgiving of slightly inaccurate measurements.

This house was built for the tufted titmouse, and the match is ideal. Tufted titmice are cavity-nesting songbirds who look for preexisting cavities, such as holes in trees. Given the ongoing decimation of woodlands, a log cabin birdhouse can be the perfect substitute.

Tufted titmice are generally confined in range to east of the Rockies. But you can find many related species, such as the crested titmouse, in the west of the country. They are a fairly small songbird with a distinctive repetitive song, gray and white coloring, with a light shadow of orange brown on their chest, and a slight crest or tuft. They are especially fond of feeders, and any reliable source of bird seed—especially sunflower seeds—will go a long way toward enticing these charmers into your yard.

Titmice line their nests with animal hair, so there's no need to add wood shavings or any other bedding material when you hang or mount the house. If you want to make this homey construction even more woodsy, you can glue pine needles and twigs to the roof and scattered on the front porch.

TOOLS & MATERIALS

Tape measure

Carpenter's pencil

Table saw

1" × 8" cedar board

Sandpaper

Waterproof wood glue

Silicone sealant

Hammer

6d 1½" galvanized casing nails

Clamps

Power drill & bits

1¼" Forstner bit or spade bit
or hole saw

Jigsaw or miter saw

Speed square

1½" exterior screws

1 × 6" white vinyl perforated
plumbing strap

Paintbrush

Dark brown exterior wood stain

(2) eye screws

Chain or steel wire

CUT LIST

(38) ¾ × ¾ × 6" logs
(1) ¾ × 6¾ × 8" long roof
(1) ¾ × 6 × 8" short roof
(1) ¾ × 6 × 8" floor

TUFTED TITMOUSE LOG CABIN

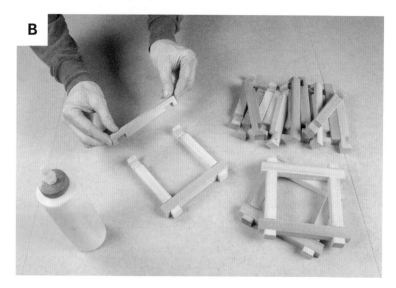

1 Cut all the pieces to the dimensions on the cut list, and cut a cleanout door in the floor. Cut square rods of ¾" cedar longer than the 6" specified in the project. Mark the end of one of the long strips for a 6" crosscut. Then, mark ⅜" deep × ¾" wide laps on this marked segment, insetting these lap cuts ⅜" from the ends. Cut the laps on a table saw with a standard blade, backing the work piece up against the miter gauge with a scrap fence attached to it [**fig. A**]. Once the first laps are cut, crosscut the first log at the 6" mark and use it as a template to repeat the process to create 27 more logs with lap cuts in them.

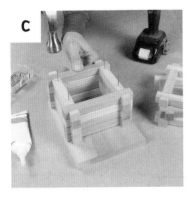

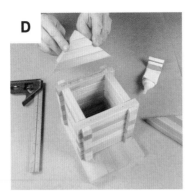

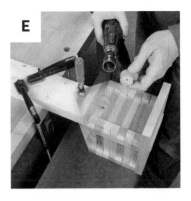

2 Cut 10 more logs to length but without the lap cuts. These will be used for the gable ends and to decorate the porch.

3 Use sandpaper or a file to ease the sharp edges of each of the 38 logs to help simulate roughhewn timbers. Doing this will enhance the realism of the cabin.

4 Group the logs by fours to form the stacked, interlocking layers of the cabin. Attach the logs of each layer with dabs of waterproof wood glue in the lapped areas and by interlocking the joints [**fig. B**].

5 Use silicone sealant to fasten the first layer to the floor over the cleanout door area and so that the ends of the logs are flush with the back and side edges of the floor. Nail this layer to floor using galvanized casing nails.

6 Stack six more layers on top of the first one, keeping their edges aligned and checking for uniformity often with a square. Attach each layer with sealant and four galvanized casing nails. Alternate the nail locations from front and back to side to side with each layer and be sure to keep the nails located near the corners on the front wall of the cabin, because it will still require an entry hole [**fig. C**]. (The nails must be clear of the entry hole location.)

7 Using waterproof wood glue, create two blanks of four logs each for the gabled ends of the roof. Make sure the faces and ends of the logs are flush and clamp these blanks together until the glue dries.

8 Draw a centerline across each gable blank. Use this as a reference for marking two 45° angles that form the roof pitch. Cut the angles on the gables with a miter, table, or jigsaw.

9 Attach a gable end to the front and back walls of the cabin with silicone sealant. Make sure the sharp ends of the gables align with the ends of the cabin logs [**fig. D**].

10 Mark the center point for the entry hole. Insert a backup board inside the cabin to help ensure a clean cut on the backside of the front wall when boring the entry hole. Bore the entry hole with a 1¼" Forstner bit, hole saw, or spade bit [**fig. E**].

11 Glue and screw the roof panels along their long edges to form the roof peak using wood glue and 1½" exterior screws.

12 Glue and screw the roof to the cabin, centering it front to back. Attach the two porch logs to the floor with sealant.

13 Stain the birdhouse and install the two screw eyes at the roof peak for hanging. Install the cleanout door on the project with plastic or galvanized metal perforated straps and exterior screws.

The prothonotary warbler is one of the most stunning species of warbler. It's easy to spot no matter where it lands.

There are few designs that can rival this one for pure, over-the-top graphic style and personality. Crafted with fun and lively decorative elements that evoke a true fisherman's lodging, this birdhouse is not only truly unique, it offers a big splash of bold color to your backyard.

The same can be said of the intended occupant of this house. Warblers are a group of about fifty species ranging all across the United States. It is an incredibly diverse family with colors ranging from arresting black-and-white designs to simply jaw-dropping all-yellow birds with showy color contrasts. But almost all warblers offer a real benefit to the homeowner who enjoys a little backyard time: lyrical and pleasing song.

Be aware that you may not be able to attract some warblers as lodgers simply because some species of warbler are open-nesters and won't make use of a house. Others, though, will gladly take a seaside free rental.

Most warblers are insect eaters, but many eat fruits and nuts as well. All warblers, however, are fond of water. You'll have much more luck inviting them in if your yard is larger or close to a substantial body of water.

Different warblers prefer different habitats and have different habits. Some, such as the yellow warbler, spend most of their time high up in tree branches. Others, such as the equally colorful prothonotary warbler, prefer marshlands and watery areas, where they can search the underbrush for delicious creepy crawly meals. No matter which type you're dealing with, keep in mind that these are skittish birds who don't necessarily welcome a lot of human interaction; it's best to enjoy them at a distance.

Given how boldly colored this birdhouse is, that should not be a problem. The structure includes small decorations that reinforce the nautical theme, including an anchor on the front of the house and a faux life preserver on the side—there's even a steamship stack as a chimney! You can change up the color scheme as you see fit, but given the decorations, it's probably best to stick with bolder hues. And avoid painting the roof dark colors or you risk overheating the interior of the birdhouse.

TOOLS & MATERIALS

Tape measure

Carpenter's pencil

1 × 8" pine board (or substitute ¾" exterior plywood)

¼" balsa wood board

Circular or table saw

Power drill & bits

1¼" Forstner bit

1" wood dowel

Miter saw

Waterproof wood glue

1½" galvanized finish nails

2" deck crews

(2) 2" brass butt hinges

¾" brass hook catch

Wood putty

Putty knife

Sandpaper

1" paintbrush

Model-building brush

Exterior flat navy blue paint

Exterior gloss white paint

Exterior black model paint

Painter's tape

Utility knife or woodworker's carving tool

Silicone adhesive

1½" seal locknut or 1" conduit locknut

1¼" seal locknut or 1" conduit locknut

White plastic curtain ring

Screw eyes (optional)

Chain (optional)

Mounting post (optional)

CUT LIST

(1) ¾ × 4½ × 4½" floor

(1) ¾ × 3 × 6" rear gable

(1) ¾ × 6 × 10½" front

(1) ¾ × 4½ × 7½" back

(2) ¾ × 5¼ × 7½" sides

(1) ¾ × 6¾ × 8" wide roof

(1) ¾ × 6 × 8" narrow roof

(1) 1 × 3" dowel smokestack

HOW TO BUILD A
WARBLER'S SEASIDE RETREAT

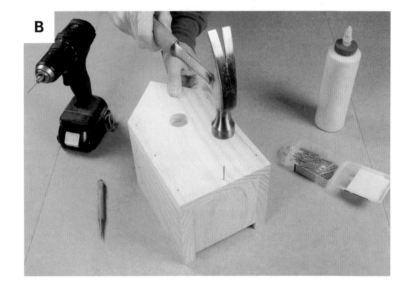

1 Cut all the pieces to the dimensions on the cut list. Mark and cut the triangle for a rear gable with a 6" base, 4¼"sides, and a 90° top angle. Drill three ¼" holes centered side to side and about 1" down from one 4½" edge of each side wall.

2 Measure and mark the center of the entry hole on the front 6" up from the bottom and centered side to side. Drill out the entry hole with a 1¼" Forstner bit.

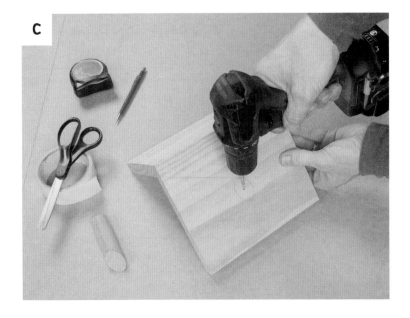

C

3 Cut a 3½" long smokestack from a 1¼" dowel. Miter the bottom to 45° (the smokestack cants slightly toward the back of the birdhouse) [**fig. A**].

4 Drill pilot holes and glue and nail one short side of a side wall to an edge of the floor using 1½" galvanized finishing nails. Repeat with the opposite side wall. (Make sure the side-wall ventilation holes are at the top of the wall, opposite the floor.)

5 Drill pilot holes and glue and nail one short side of the front to a short edge of the floor and the side wall edges, precisely overlapping the side walls [**fig. B**].

6 Drill pilot holes and glue and nail the two roof panels together along their short edges, with the wider panel overlapping the edge of the other panel [**fig. C**]. Position the smokestack on the roof and outline the base to mark the location. Drill a pilot hole centered in the marked area, down through the roof.

7 Position the back gable at the back of the house, drill piltot holes, and screw it to the side wall on each side [**fig. D**].

8 Position the back flush under the rear gable and mark for the hinges along the joint between the two. Mark the position of the hook catch on the bottom of the back wall and the underside of the floor. Drill pilot holes for the hinge screws and the latch and catch in all surfaces.

D

9 Carefully position the roof so that it overhangs the front gable by 1". Drill pilot holes and screw the roof to the gables.

10 Putty over all the screw heads and imperfections and sand smooth. Paint the birdhouse body navy blue and the roof bright white. Paint the smokestack with a navy blue strip at the bottom, a bright white middle stripe, and a black stripe at the top [**fig. E**].

11 Screw the roof to the smokestack through the predrilled hole. Screw the hinges to the back gable and to the back wall, through the predrilled holes. Screw the hook and catch to the bottom of the back wall and underside of the floor, respectively, using the predrilled holes [**fig. F**].

12 Use painter's tape to paint four stripes equidistant around the plastic curtain ring to make the life preserver. Use a utility knife or woodworker's carving tool to cut out the anchor shape using the illustration on page 85 as your guide. Paint the anchor black with oil-based model paint and then use wood glue to attach it at the base of the front beneath the portal entry hole. Attach the life preserver to the side wall in the same way.

E

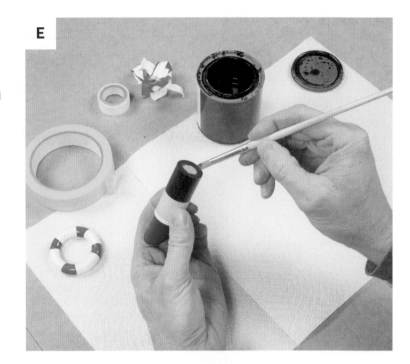

F

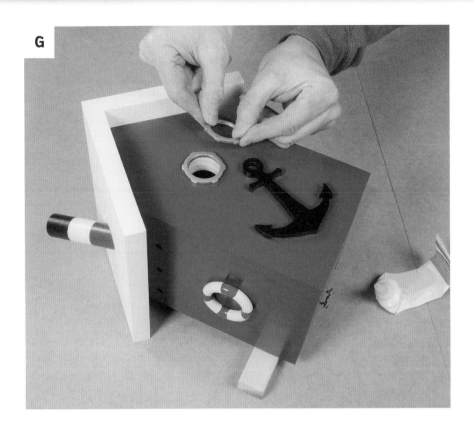

G

13 Use silicone adhesive to attach the 1½" locknut around the entry hole (for a more authentic look, you can paint the locknuts gold, so they look like actual brass marine fittings). Attach the 1¼" locknut right next to the entry hole as if it were an open portal window [**fig. G**]. Use screw eyes and chain to hang the house or, preferably, mount it on its own post. In either case, the house should be about 7' above the ground, with a clear line of sight all around.

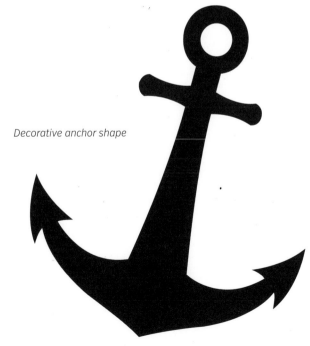

Decorative anchor shape

The American robin is one of the prettier songbirds you can invite into your yard, and they are low-maintenance tenants.

Do you have leftover flowerpots from your container garden? Why not put one to good use housing a lovely and no-fuss songbird in your yard? The simple flowerpot nesting-box project here is a great way to recycle unused garden containers and is easy to build. It's an unexpected look in yard, and you can customize the flowerpot in a number of ways to make the project really stand out. Paint the pot an eye-catching color and play around with painting the wood insert that fronts the nesting box. The robins will happily use it whatever the look!

You shouldn't have much problem attracting lodgers for this flowerpot. Robins are ubiquitous across the country and are fairly easy to please. They eat a wide range of insects and fruits. If you have a diverse landscape and a fruit tree or bush, it's likely a robin will feel at home in your yard.

These can be exceptionally fun birds to watch. They skitter along the ground looking for fallen berries and hidden insects, and if you're lucky enough to have robins in the yard during mating season, you see some fairly amusing behavior during courtship (they even do a type of open-billed kiss). If you have honeysuckle in your yard, you'll be treated to the sight of tipsy robins after they eat the berries.

Although they have a varied diet, robins will eagerly take advantage of a feeder in the yard. But do keep in mind that they are lawn foragers. Any chemical fertilizers, lawn food, weed-and-feed products, or other synthetic materials can have a very serious effect on the health of robins you've attracted to your yard.

Where the flowerpot is concerned, don't hesitate to go a bit wild with decorations. Terra cotta takes paint well, and a bright and cheery scheme might add vibrance to any garden. You can also stencil on the pot quite easily, allowing you to add whimsical labels, fun figures, and even a naturalistic flower to really make the lodging fit in with its surroundings.

HOW TO BUILD A
ROBIN'S FLOWERPOT

TOOLS & MATERIALS

10" terra cotta flowerpot

Carpenter's pencil

Carpenter's compass or trammel

½" exterior grade plywood

Straightedge

Power drill & bits

Jigsaw

Sandpaper

1" paintbrush

Dark exterior wood stain (optional)

Miter saw

1" deck screws

Silicone adhesive

CUT LIST

(1) ½ × 5" (radius) half circle insert

(1) ½ × 6" dia. base (approx.)

(1) ¾ × 1 × 8" brace (approx.)

A

B

1 Measure the inside width of the pot's mouth. Use a carpenter's compass or a trammel to trace a circle to match that measurement on a scrap piece of ½" exterior grade plywood. Draw a center line bisecting the circle and then draw a line parallel to, and 1½" below the line [**fig. A**].

2 Drill three holes along the arc of what will be the bottom of the insert, about 1" apart. Drill an access hole and use a jigsaw to cut out the arc with the lower line as the top edge of the half-moon shape. Sand the edges of the insert [**fig. B**].

3 Stand the pot on a second piece of plywood and trace the bottom. Cut out this circle with a jigsaw, following about 1/16" inside the traced line. Sand the edges to about a 14° bevel on one side (to conform to the slope of the pot). Check that it fits inside the pot, flush to the bottom, without jamming. Stain one side of the half-moon piece with a dark stain if you prefer. It can also be left natural.

4 Drill a 1/4" reference hole in the center of the wood disc that will sit inside the pot [**fig. C**].

5 Miter the ends of the brace to 14°. Screw one end of the brace to the base disc as close to the edge of the disc as possible. Dot silicone adhesive on the outside face of the wood disc and place it in the base of the pot with the brace pointing up. Position the arc in place in the mouth of the pot. Press the brace down to better follow the angled side of the pot and adjust the arc so that the end of the brace contacts the arc as close to the radial point as possible [**fig. D**].

6 Drill a pilot hole and screw the base of the half-moon to the brace with a 1" deck screw. Remove the wood from the pot.

7 Lightly sand the inside edge of pot's lip. Lay a light bead of silicone adhesive around the bottom of the pot and along the lip where the arc will rest. Slip the base and arc into place, and hold there for a minute, to give the adhesive a little time to set [**fig. E**].

8 Mount the flowerpot about 8' above the ground by drilling a starter hole and driving a lag screw with a fender washer through the hole in the base disc and into a sturdy post, the side of a shed, or a large sturdy tree.

The house finch boasts stunningly beautiful chest plumage in shades of fire. The bird's song is even lovelier.

A liberal take on the old English thatched-roof public house (or pub), this project is an extremely unusual design that incorporates a living roof. Although the soil is not deep enough to grow a wide range of flowers, you can easily cultivate attractive moss, groundcovers such as sedum, and even some low grasses that may provide food for the birds when the grasses go to seed.

The decorations and actual design of the house are just as distinctive. The birdhouse has a brick base courtesy of model-making brick sheet. A balsa wood front door creates a convincing illusion that a pint waits just inside. The structure of the house can be embellished even more with a few additional model-making supplies (see the optional last step) and a little bit of imagination.

Regardless of how you personalize the design, house finches are going to be drawn to it as a comfortable and alluring home. The roof helps keep the interior a nice even temperature, and house finches aren't particular in any case. They are in fact durable, adaptable, and prolific breeders. Until about 1940, their populations were limited to the west coast and parts of Mexico. Then, they were introduced into the wild on Long Island (originally stocked as pet birds, but they did not sell and were consequently freed or discarded, depending on how you look at it). From that point, their numbers increased and the birds spread to almost ever state in the union.

Fortunately, the distinctive blush coloring on the chest and head of the male house finch makes it an incredibly attractive bird. Oddly enough, the coloring is a by-product of the bird's vegetarian diet. Even prettier, though, is the house finch's song. It is a truly lovely stereotypical songbird call, delicate and musical.

This is a very friendly bird that normally won't be put off by human presence in the yard. They are attracted to feeders, especially those stocked with oily, high-quality seed mixes. And don't be fooled by the theme of this birdhouse—house finches stick to water during happy hour.

TOOLS & MATERIALS

Tape measure

Carpenter's pencil

Speed square

Circular or table saw

½" exterior plywood

¾" exterior plywood

⅛ × 3" balsa wood plank

Miter saw

Power drill & bits

Waterproof wood glue

1" screws

Masking tape

Bar clamps

1⅝" Forstner bit

Sandpaper

1½" deck screws

Wood putty

Putty knife

Model paintbrush

1" paintbrush

Exterior glass white paint

Blue oil-based model paint

Waterproof dark brown wood stain

Exterior silicone adhesive

Brick sheet for modeling

Letter stencils

Gold oil-based model paint

6 mil. plastic sheet or similar moisture barrier

Potting soil

Moss or sedum starts

continued on page 94

HOW TO BUILD
FINCH'S PUB

1 Cut all the pieces to the dimensions on the cut list. Miter one end of each roof frame side to 70°. Bevel one end of each roof panel to 70°. Cut one end of the front and back walls to a 140° point. Bevel one 6" end of each side to 20° [**fig. A**].

2 Drill pilot holes and glue and screw the roof frame sections to the top of each roof panel [**fig. B**].

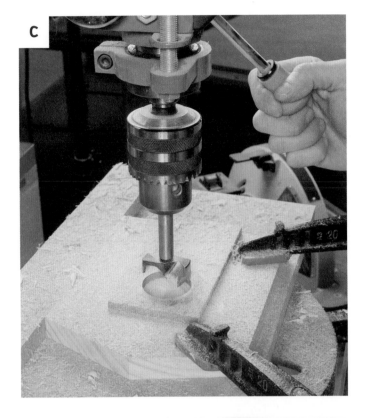

C

3 Drill pilot holes and glue and screw the two roof sections together through the frame side miters. Drive 1" screws both ways to hold the joint securely (this does not need to support the roof over the long term because it will be fastened to the body of the birdhouse for structural support).

4 Measure and mark the door placement on the front. (The door should be centered side to side and flush with the bottom of the front.) Temporarily tape the door in place on the front. Turn the front over and clamp it to a scrap piece. Measure and mark the center of the entry hole 4½" up from the bottom of the front and centered side to side. Use a 1⅝" Forstner bit to drill the entry hole down through the front and the door [**fig. C**].

5 Remove the door and sand the entry hole edges in the door and the front to ensure they're smooth.

6 Drill pilot holes and glue and screw one side wall to one long edge of the floor using 1½" deck screws. Drill pilot holes and glue and screw the front to the floor and the side. Repeat the process to fasten the back to the floor and side [**fig. D**].

7 Putty over all the screw heads and sand them smooth. Paint the birdhouse body and one face of the remaining side with white exterior, oil-based paint. Paint one face and the edges of the balsa wood door blue. Stain the outside surfaces and underside of the roof frame dark brown.

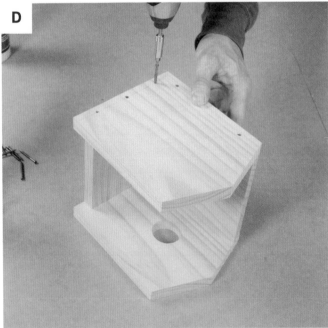

D

TOOLS & MATERIALS

continued from page 92

Fine chicken wire or coarse bird netting

Staple gun & staples

(2) 1" stainless-steel butt hinges

Stainless-steel hook clasp

Screwdriver (optional)

Mounting post

CUT LIST

(4) ¾ × 1 × 5⅞" roof frame sides

(2) ¾ × 1 × 9" roof frame ends

(2) ½ × 5½ × 10½" roof panels

(2) ¾ × 6 × 7¼" sides

(2) ¾ × 6½ × 8⅛" front & back

(1) ½ × 5 × 6" floor

(1) ⅛ × 3 × 6" balsa wood door

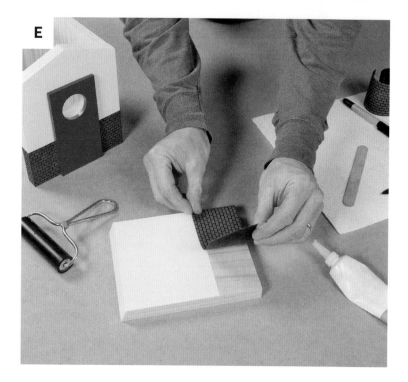

E

8 Lightly sand where the door will be glued over the entry hole. Coat the back of the door with silicone adhesive and press it into place on the front. Cut a 2½" strip of brick sheet to fit on either side of the door along the bottom of the front. Sand the area to give it some tooth and then coat the back of the brick sheet sections with silicone adhesive and stick them in place [**fig. E**]. Clamp the door and brick sheet until the adhesive has cured.

9 Follow the same process to line the bottom edge of the attached side with brick sheet, clamping it until the adhesive sets. Line the unattached side with the brick sheet in the same way.

10 Use letter stencils (available in a range of styles at crafts stores and online) to paint the words Finch's Pub in gold lettering centered over the door.

11 Drill pilot holes and glue and screw the roof in place to the front, back, and side wall so that the roof overhangs the front (use 1½" deck screws on the back because you'll need to drive the screws through the frame and down into the back).

12 Cut a 10½ × 8½" piece of thick plastic sheet. Coat the inside surfaces of the frame with silicone adhesive and press the plastic down into the adhesive (there should be a slight overlap on the top of the frame all around—glue it down to the top edges) [**fig. F**]. Put bags of dried beans or similar weights inside the roof frame to hold the plastic in place while the adhesive cures.

F

G

13 Pack potting soil into the roof, leaving about ¼" of space at the top. Slightly moisten the sphagnum moss and pack a sparse layer on top of the soil. Cut a section of chicken wire to fit across the frame and staple it to the top edges all around. Trim off any excess with shears [**fig. G**].

14 Put the second side wall in position. Mark the locations of the two 1" butt hinges on the wall and the underside of the roof and the hook clasp on the bottom edge of the wall and the underside of the floor. Remove the wall and screw the hinges and hook clasp in place and screw the clasp lock to the floor. Replace the side wall and screw the hinges to the roof.

15 Use a screwdriver or similar tool to poke planting holes down through the chicken wire and moss and into the soil. Plant sedum, trailing perennials, or moss plugs (it's best to use mature starts). Water lightly when you're done.

Optional: You can dress the design up even more like a pub by using model-making supplies that can be found at crafts stores, online, and at model railroading shops. For instance, glue faux miniature shrubs along each side or use tiny model kegs cut in half lengthwise and glued to the brick front. You can also paint pub windows on the sides or front or add signage, such as Free Beer.

16 Mount the house on a sturdy post 10' (3.0 m) above the ground, with a clear line of sight in all directions. Alternatively, you can screw the house to a large tree trunk or even a sturdy fence. Just keep in mind this is a fairly heavy house when you consider the weight of the wet soil and plants on top.

SPARROW MILK CARTON

Although far from the most colorful songbird, the sparrow will make itself known by both its aggressive behavior toward other songbirds and its appealing song.

There is a trend among amateur crafters to repurpose old milk cartons as birdhouses. Unfortunately, while these flimsy structures may be easy to decorate, they are far less than ideal as lodgings for a bird family. This project takes its cue from those efforts, with a shape that mimics the standard half-gallon (1.9 L) milk carton. But this birdhouse is much sturdier and well adapted to the needs of a songbird, such as the ubiquitous house sparrow.

The sparrow is not native to America, having been introduced in 1850. However, you wouldn't know it was an immigrant by the way sparrow populations have spread across the country. Partly, that's a result of their aggressiveness. House sparrows will hurt or even kill adults and fledglings of other small bird species just to take over a nesting site. It's why many backyard birders sometimes take drastic steps to prevent sparrows from calling the yard their home.

The unique and distinctive design of this birdhouse takes a different tack. You can use this structure as a highly visible bait-and-switch, in concert with other birdhouses in your yard. It will provide a nesting site away from other songbirds.

You can maintain this separation by placing the Sparrow Milk Carton close to your house; sparrows are very comfortable around humans. And, if you want to keep the sparrows out of your general bird feeder, limit the seed mix to safflower and Nyjer seeds, neither of which sparrows like.

Creating the unique shape of the box entails using some unusual materials and techniques. The sides are formed of cut-and-bent sheet metal. Most of the metal work can be done with basic tools; if you don't have an angle grinder to cut and debur the sheet metal, you can use heavy-duty tin snips and an inexpensive deburring tool.

The project includes a cleanout door built into the floor. It doesn't require a more complete door or easier access because there's no reason to check on the sparrow eggs or nestlings during fledging. Just clean out the box between broods. (The cleanout door is simply held in place with a sheet metal strap and two screws.) You can choose another color for the milk carton, but keep in mind that darker colors may cause the box to retain more heat and become uncomfortably hot—a risk with any metal-sided birdhouse.

TOOLS & MATERIALS

Tape measure

Straight edge

Speed square

1 × 1 × 18" cedar board

Marker & carpenter's pencil

Circular or table saw

Miter saw (optional)

Power drill & bits

1¼" Forstner bit

12 × 24" 26-gauge sheet metal

Metal scribe

Aviation snips, or angle grinder with cutting wheel & grinding wheel

Deburring tool (optional)

Bench vise

(3) Scrap 2 × 4s, one with an edge beveled to 45°

½" panhead screws

½" stainless steel wood screws

Silicone sealant

Bar clamps, various sizes

Putty knife

Grommet kit & ⅜" grommets

Degreasing cleanser

Emery cloth

Paintbrush

Waterproof metal primer & topcoat

Waterproof wood primer & topcoat

Letter stencils (optional)

CUT LIST

(2) ¾ × 5 × 10" front & back

(2) ¾ × 2 × 3½" bottom cleats

(1) ¾ × 3½ × 3½" floor

(2) ¾ × 2½ × 5" carton-top ends

(1) ¾ × 1⅜ × 2¾" top brace

(2) 5 × 16¼" sheet metal sides

(1) 1½ × 5" sheet metal cleanout strap

HOW TO BUILD A
SPARROW MILK CARTON

1 Cut the wood pieces to the dimensions on the cut list. Mark one carton-top end blank with a triangle, with a 5" side as the base and a 90° point centered on the opposite side [**fig. A**]. Cut out the triangle and use it as a template to mark the second carton-top end. Bevel the bases of both triangles to 45°.

2 Measure and mark the front for the entry hole. The hole should be centered side to side and 6½" up from the bottom. Drill the hole with a 1¼" Forstner bit.

3 Cut the sheet metal sides following the diagrams on page 156 by scribing the cut lines and making the cuts with aviation snips (as an alternative, use an angle grinder fit with a cutting wheel). Debur and smooth the edges with a deburring tool, or the grinder, using a coarse grinding disc. Measure and mark the bend lines on both sheet metal sides. Mark and cut the cleanout strap to size [**fig. B**].

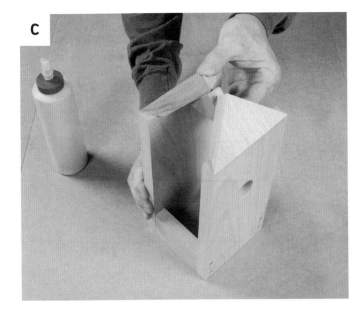

4 Drill pilot holes and screw the front to one long end of the floor using ½" stainless steel wood screws. Attach the back to the floor in the same fashion. With the frame lying on edge, position the front and back carton-top ends on top of the front and back. Position the top brace triangle between the two carton-top ends so that the points of each end almost touch. Glue the triangle and top ends in place. Mark the outside of the ends for screws into the triangle [**fig. C**].

5 Once the glue has dried, drill pilot holes at the marks. Screw the bracket to the front and back with ½" stainless-steel screws. Repeat with the back and the second triangular top piece.

6 Make the sheet metal bends by clamping a side between two 2 × 4 scraps, positioned along the bend line. Bend the metal with a third scrap 2 × 4, pressing along the bend line until you reach the appropriate angle — roughly 36°. Periodically check the bend against the wood subassembly you've fabricated. Repeat with the second side once all the bends are made for the first side.

7 Drill two ⅜" hanging holes 2" apart, centered side to side and top to bottom on the 1½" top flange. Transfer the hole marks to the exact same location on the second side and drill the holes in that side.

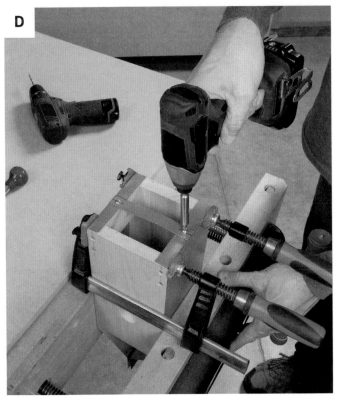

8 Begin attaching one side by hooking the bottom bend along one open edge of the floor. Mark the bottom overlap of the sheet metal for a screw centered side to side, and drill a pilot hole through the metal into the floor. Position the cleanout strap with one end hole overlapping the pilot hole and screw both the strap and the side bottom flap to the underside of the floor with a ½" stainless-steel wood screw [**fig. D**]. Mark screw locations about 1" on either side of the first screw and drill pilot holes at those locations. Drive screws into those holes. Repeat the process with the opposite side.

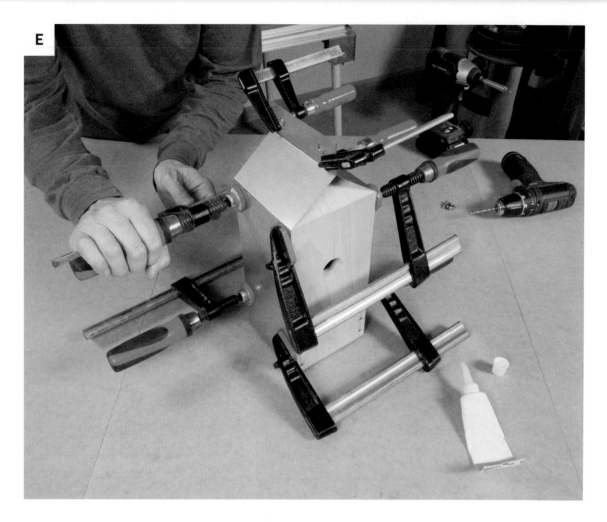

E

9 Put the floor in position, secured by the clean-out strap. Coat the edges of the front and back, including the carton-top end edges, with a silicone sealant. Coat the inner surfaces of the top of the sides with the sealant. Clamp the sheet metal sides to the wood frame and at the top. Use a putty knife to remove any squeeze out and allow the adhesive to cure completely before proceeding [**fig. E**].

10 Mark three holes, along the top, middle, and bottom of the front and back edges. Drill pilot holes through the sheet metal and into the frame edges at the marked locations. Screw the sides to the front and back edges with ½" panhead screws. Use a grommet kit to insert ⅜" grommets into both hanging holes in the top flange [**fig. F**].

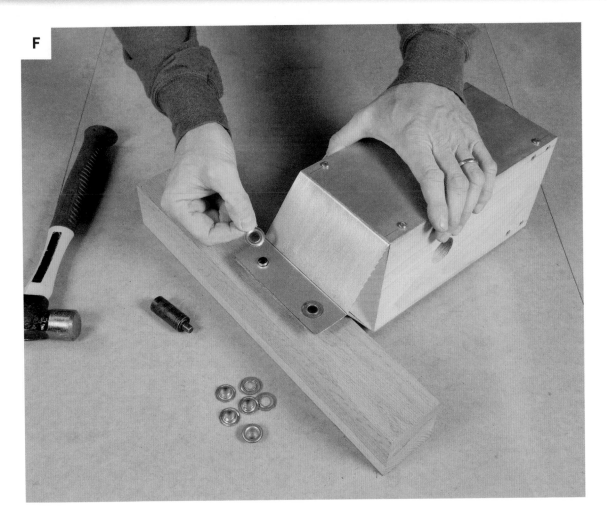

F

11 Clean the metal surfaces thoroughly with a degreasing cleanser. Rough up the surfaces with an emery cloth and prime with a metal primer. Prime the wood with a wood exterior primer. Paint the metal with a bright white topcoat of metal paint and paint the wood with a bright white exterior, oil-based paint. Stencil the word "Milk" on each side, if desired. Hang the birdhouse from a sturdy branch or overhang, 8 to 15" (2.4 to 4.6 m) above the ground, with a clear line of sight all around.

LARGE BIRD SHELTERS

IT'S NOT JUST SONGBIRDS THAT NEED eye-catching places to stay; larger predators can also use a home on the way to wherever they're going. The creations in this chapter are bigger canvases on which you can exercise your creativity. The designs offered here are a bit more sedate than others in the book, but they lend themselves well to customization and personalization.

If you're not quite sure about inviting in larger or more secretive birds, you might want to consider that most of the birds for which the projects in this chapter were developed are known for hunting vermin and larger pests, such as rats, mice, and voles. They are also some of the most impressive birds to watch, when you get a chance to actually see them in action.

You can paint, stencil, or modify the outside of these boxes to suit your own tastes. However, it's a good idea not to radically change the interior dimensions of the nesting boxes here because larger birds tend to need the space. Features such as climbing ladders are also essential for fledglings, so make sure you incorporate those no matter how you change the look of the project.

Mourning doves are open nesters rather than cavity roosters. Although they can turn a sturdy branch into a home, they welcome the confines and mild protection of a roosting ledge such as the one in this project.

It's okay to have a bit of fun at a bird's expense, as long as the bird doesn't catch on. That's the inspiration for this whimsical nesting ledge design. Fortunately, this monster bares its fangs but never bites.

The ledge is meant to accommodate a pair of nesting doves. Mourning doves are perhaps the most common and abundant game bird in America. They are essentially the opposite of endangered because although hunters kill tens of millions of mourning doves every year, the remaining population in the United States is estimated at 350 million. The birds can be found in all the lower 48 states, as well as parts of Canada and throughout Mexico. Known for its melancholy cooing, mourning doves are relatively large birds with understated grey-and-brown plumage and a gentle nature.

Mourning doves are almost exclusively ground feeders, and you can help them out in that regard with a scattering of seed. Fortunately, they will quickly vacuum up seeds that other birds may not like, such as milo, cracked corn, and even weed seed, but they also like sunflower seeds. A source of water is also crucial. A pair of breeding mourning doves will need about two and half acres to themselves, and these birds are skittish. They are easy prey for cats because they tend to scour the ground for seeds. If you have outdoor cats, it's probably a good idea to let the birds roost elsewhere.

Mourning doves are open nesters, making this project an easy construction for even very novice woodworkers. The design is actually very forgiving and can be adapted for a different wood or a slightly different look. The hardest part is the half-circle in each side. These are simpler to cut than they may appear; craft one side and use it as a template for the second.

The cedar used in the construction is an ideal choice for a nesting box or ledge. Not only will the wood look good now and in the future, it will also endure insect attacks and long-term sun exposure. There really is no need to finish the ledge. But if you do, carefully avoid getting any finish on the roosting surfaces. You can build on the idea behind the design by using a cheaper wood, such as plywood, and painting the exterior to really look like a monster. You could even glue on some faux fur!

TOOLS & MATERIALS

Tape measure

Speed square

Carpenter's pencil

1 × 8" cedar board

⅛ × 3 × 12" balsa wood plank

Circular or table saw

Utility knife or coping saw

Model paintbrush

1" paintbrush

Exterior gloss white paint

Black oil-based model paint

Power drill & bits

Carpenter's compass (or substitute a trammel or pencil & string)

Clamps

Jigsaw

Waterproof wood glue

1½" deck screws

2" deck screws

Wood putty

Putty knife

Sandpaper

Natural, no-VOC finish (optional)

CUT LIST

(2) ¾ × 7¼ × 9½" sides

(1) ¾ × 1 × 7¼" front lip

(1) ¾ × 7¼ × 10¼" back

(1) ¾ × 7¼ × 8" bottom

(1) ¾ × 7¼ × 10" roof

(2) ¾ × 1 × 1" eye mounting blocks

HOW TO BUILD A
MOURNING DOVE MONSTER LEDGE

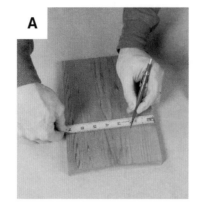

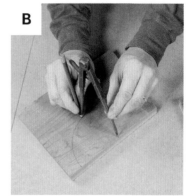

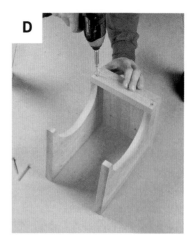

1 Cut the cedar to the dimensions on the cut list. Cut a 10° bevel on one short edge of the back and on both short edges of the roof (oriented in the same direction).

2 Use a utility knife or coping saw to cut out balsa eyes and teeth shapes as shown in the illustration on page 157. Paint the shapes white and paint black irises on the eyes.

3 Drill ¼" drainage holes at each corner of the floor about 2" in from each edge. Drill two ½" hanging holes through the back, 3" down from the beveled edge and 2" in from each long edge [**fig. A**].

4 Finish a side by cutting one end to a 10° angle. Measure and mark 4" down the long edge from the front of the angle cut. Use a carpenter's compass or a trammel to mark a half circle with a 3⅜" radius, with the point held at the mark

you made on the edge [**fig. B**]. Clamp the side down and cut out the half circle with a jigsaw. Use this side as a template to trace the cuts on the second side.

5 Drill pilot holes and glue and screw the floor to the bottom of one side with 1½" deck screws. The uncut short edge of the side should be flush along the long edge of the floor (the uncut back of the side should be flush with what will be the back of the floor). Repeat the process with the opposite side. [**fig. C**].

6 Position the front lip on edge across the front edges of the sides. Drill pilot holes and glue and screw the lip to the sides with 2" deck screws [**fig. D**].

7 Position the back so that the top bevel is flush with the side wall angle cuts. Drill pilot holes and glue and screw the back to the sides and the floor with 2" deck screws.

8 Set the roof in place so that one edge bevel is flush to the back face of the back and the sides are flush to the outside faces of the sides. Drill pilot holes and glue and screw the roof to the sides and back with 2" deck screws [**fig. E**].

9 Glue the eye-mounting blocks to the back of each eye, flush with the bottom of each eye and centered side to side. (The blocks should be invisible from the front.) Decide on the best location for the eyes on top of the roof and then drill pilot holes down though the top of each one into the roof.

10 Putty over the screw heads and sand smooth. Use a natural, no-VOC finish or leave unfinished. Lightly sand the front of the lip and the front edge of the roof where the teeth will be placed (the top teeth should be flush with the top of the roof and flush with the outside edges; the bottom teeth should be flush with the bottom edge and centered side to side). Coat the back of the teeth with wood glue, and glue them in place.

11 Mount the ledge in the crotch of a tree, between 8 and 10" above the ground. Secure it in place by wiring through the holes in the back and around the tree trunk.

KESTREL LODGE HOUSE

If you're going to make a cool birdhouse, you might as well make it a "home." That's the idea behind the design tweaks on this structure meant to house the fascinating feathered hunters known as raptors—specifically the small American kestrel. The birdhouse includes a paint scheme that mimics a stereotypical neighborhood home, with shutters and a chimney that add to the illusion. (The design omits the fireplace inside because birds are just not good fire builders!)

The American kestrel is a small raptor—birds that hunt their food. Sometimes called a sparrow hawk, the kestrel is actually a falcon. Although you'll need a fairly large yard if you're going to attract kestrels—and any property bordering a wetland or with a large body of water close by is even better—inviting a raptor such as this into your yard means that any rodent population will quickly diminish.

That's because kestrels hunt mice, rats, and small snakes. On the flip side, they will also just as gladly feast on chipmunks, squirrels, rabbits, and even small dogs and cats. That lack of discernment is why you should keep pets inside if you have a kestrel lodging in your yard. However, no yard is safe for raptors if you regularly use insecticides, pesticides, or put out poison for rats or mice. There is a good possibility those chemicals could adversely affect the birds and their offspring.

Put out a kestrel house no later than January to be ready when the raptors are. A kestrel house should be clean and preferably lined with a couple inches of wood shavings. Place it in a fairly open habitat with multiple perching opportunities nearby. Use a predator baffle to stop squirrels from nesting in the box and be ready to clear off starlings and sparrows who will gladly occupy the

An American kestrel in flight is a stunning sight.

box before raptors have a chance to settle in it. The wilder the surroundings appear, the better, although if you mow the lawn, kestrels can more easily spot prey rodents.

There is no need to monitor the box during brooding, but do clean it after the kestrels have moved on. This may be a bit of a chore given that the birds defecate messily inside the nest box, but it is essential. Kestrels won't nest in a dirty box in the following season.

Accommodating these birds can be well worth the effort because kestrels are dramatic and awe-inspiring in flight and majestic even when sitting, watchful, on a tree branch. They do, however, prefer a fairly quiet environment. If your backyard is regularly full of rambunctious children on play structures or if you're a social animal who hosts twice-weekly cookouts with loud music, you should consider trying to attract a different species of bird with a different birdhouse.

HARBORING HUNTERS

Be aware that while raptors, such as kestrels, may get rid of your field mouse (or mole) problem, they are just as willing to prey on songbirds. It's something to consider if you're already housing — or hope to house or feed — smaller songbirds on your property. (Of course, this can be a plus for homeowners looking to rid themselves of aggressive starling or sparrow intruders.)

HOW TO BUILD A
KESTREL LODGE HOUSE

TOOLS & MATERIALS

Tape measure

Carpenter's pencil &
permanent marker

1 × 10" pine board (or substitute
¾" exterior grade plywood)

⅛ × 3" balsa wood board

Circular or table saw

Miter saw

Speed square

Power drill & bits

2 × 2 stock (Pine is a common
choice.)

Utility knife (with a new blade)
or coping saw

Bar clamps

3" Forstner bit

1¼" deck screws

Waterproof wood glue

2" deck screws

Hammer

1½" galvanized finish nails

Wood putty

Putty knife

Sandpaper

Paintbrush

Exterior satin purple paint

Dark brown exterior wood stain

Exterior gloss white

Exterior matte black paint

continued on page 112

A

B

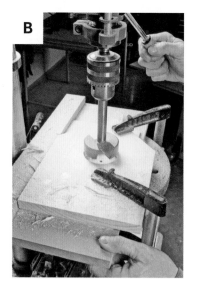

C

1 Cut the pieces for the birdhouse body and roof to the dimensions on the cut
list. Mark a 90° peak at one end of the front board using a speed square [**fig. A**]
and cut the peak with a circular saw, reserving one of the waste triangles. Bevel
one end of each side wall to 45°. Drill three ¼" ventilation holes at that end
about 1" down from the edge.

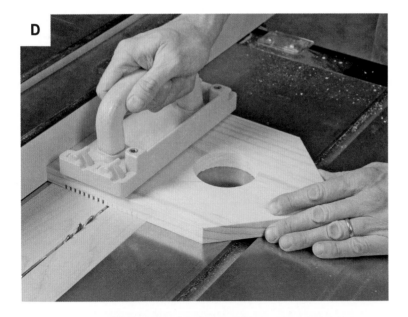

2 Cut a 3" piece of 2 × 2 stock and bevel one end to 45° for the chimney. Cut the two shutters from balsa wood using a utility knife with a new blade or a coping saw.

3 Clamp the front over a piece of scrap. Measure and mark a point 6½" from the uncut end of the front and centered side to side. Use this to center a 3" Forstner bit and drill the entry hole [**fig. B**].

4 Set the front on the back panel and align their side and bottom edges. Trace the roof profile onto the back panel. Remove the front and use the lines as reference to position the reserved cut triangle. Check that the top edges of the triangle align perfectly with the roof profile lines. Drill pilot holes and screw the triangle to the back with 1¼" stainless steel wood screws [**fig. C**].

5 Make a fledgling ladder by cutting ⅛" horizontal kerfs (slits or notches) across the inside face (the roughest face) of the front. Make the cuts starting 1" up from the uncut end and spaced every ¼" up to the bottom of the entry hole [**fig. D**]. Drill ¼" drainage holes at the corners of the floor 1" in from each edge at one end of the floor and a little more than 2" in from each side at the opposite end.

6 Align the back with the long edge of the side. Make sure the end opposite the triangle is flush with the end of the side (where the two pieces will contact the bottom). Drill pilot holes about every 2", and then glue and screw the pieces together with 2" deck screws [**fig. E**]. Repeat the process to fasten the back to the opposite side wall.

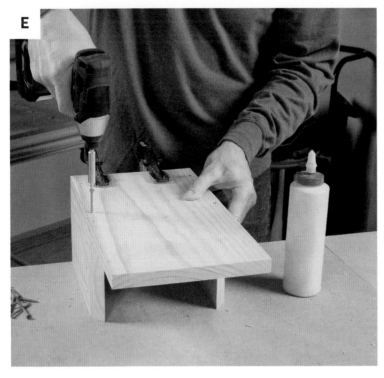

TOOLS & MATERIALS

continued from page 110

1¼" stainless-steel wood screws

Silicone sealant

(2) 2" galvanized butt hinges

Steel ruler

Permanent marker

3" deck screws

CUT LIST

(2) ¾ × 5½ × 8⅝" sides

(1) ¾ × 8¼ × 12" front

(1) ¾ × 8¼ × 15" back

(1) ¾ × 8 × 8¼"floor

(1) ¾ × 7½ × 8" short roof

(1) ¾ × 8 × 8¼" long roof

(1) ¾ × 2½ × 8" wide peak cap

(1) ¾ × 1¾ × 8" shallow peak cap

(1) 1½ × 1½ × 3" chimney

(2) ⅛ × 1½ × 3" balsa wood shutters

F

G

7 Set the front in place on the side walls. Drill pilot holes every 2" up each side of the front. Glue and nail the front to the walls with 1½" galvanized finish nails. Cover all the nail heads on the body with wood putty, let dry, and sand smooth. Paint the body of the birdhouse in an exterior mid-range purple or your favorite color (other than red).

8 Overlap the longer roof section on the edge of the shorter section along their short lengths. Drill pilot holes every 2" and fasten the two sections with wood glue and 2" deck screws. Stain the roof dark brown, except for the overlap areas where the ridge caps will be placed.

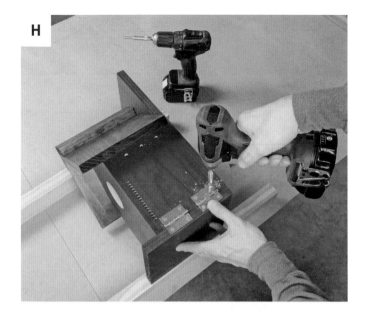

9 Paint the chimney white and paint a 1¼" square in black matte, centered on the top. Once the paint is dry, measure and mark the roof for placement. It should be centered side to side and about 2" from the edge of the narrow roof section. Glue the chimney in place then drill a pilot hole from the underside of the roof and screw the chimney to the roof [**fig. F**].

10 Glue the narrower of the roof peak caps along the roof peak opposite the butt seam, with one edge flush along the peak of the roof. Drill pilot holes about every 2" from inside the roof, and nail the peak cap in place with 1½" galvanized finish nails. Position the wider peak cap overlapping the edge of the narrow cap and fasten it in the same manner, gluing it to the roof and along the joint between the caps. Finally, drill pilot holes and nail the wider cap to the shallower along the joint [**fig. G**].

11 Lay a bead of glue along the top of the walls and the top edges of the roof support triangle on the back. Set the roof in position, Drill pilot holes and screw it in place with 1¼" stainless steel wood screws. Cover all the screw heads with putty, sand, and coat the roof and peak caps with a second coat of stain. Lay a small, neat bead of silicone sealant along the joint between the back of the roof and the back.

12 With the birdhouse lying face up, butt the floor up to the back, with the edges flush. Attach the floor to one side with two 2" butt hinges [**fig. H**]. Drill a pilot hole and use one 2" deck screw to fasten the floor to the opposite side.

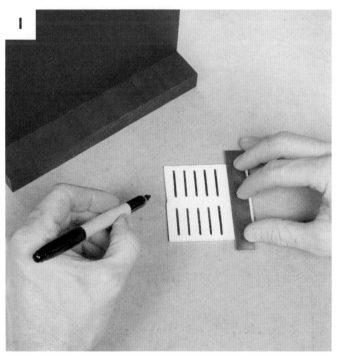

13 Paint the shutters white and use a permanent marker and a straight edge (or black paint and a tiny brush) to mark the slats on the shutters [**fig. I**]. Measure and mark the placement of the shutters and glue them in place on either side of the entry hole. Hang the birdhouse on a post, fence, or tree, at least 12 feet off the ground, by drilling two holes in the exposed portion of the back and fastening it with 3" deck screws.

BARN OWL A-FRAME

Barn owls have incredible eyesight and even better hearing. Their auditory talents allow them to successfully hunt even in complete darkness.

Unexpected shapes can be eye-catching features in a yard, and few are as eye-catching as a large A-frame structure mounted on the side of an outbuilding. Meant for a family of barn owls, this structure combines a naturally attractive design with a little bit of flair in the details. A front entrance ledge is formed by a series of dowels in a staggered formation. The roof angle and overhang will bring to mind an alpine ski lodge. The form leaves plenty of space inside for the useful and secretive occupants.

A barn owl is the farmer's friend. When owls take up residence in a barn or other outbuilding, the local rodent population quickly plummets. These nighttime hunters will feed on rats, mice, voles, gophers, and other destructive rodents. If you have a large rural property—especially if you have a suitable outbuilding, such as a large, high-ceilinged garage—you too can take advantage of this avian pest eliminator by putting up a lovely home where the predator will be comfortable during breeding season.

The barn owl's range is widespread and the bird can be found in all but the northernmost US states. Although, like all owls, this species is nocturnal, if they choose your nesting box, you'll eventually see the snow-white, heart-shaped face and ebony eyes peering down at you from a high perch. You're also likely to hear their unusual raspy cry as they hunt.

Obviously, the nest box in this project is designed to be mounted on a building. But barn owls can be discerning about where they nest. They prefer a large open area, such as grasslands or a lightly wooded region. They shy from deep forests where they might encounter their enemy and predator, the great horned owl. The actual nest site should be fairly quiet and at a remove from any significant human activity. The nest box should be placed 12 to 20 feet above ground level.

Because barn owls can see, hear, and hunt in near complete darkness, you'll make the area more attractive by removing or disabling motion lights and any other bright lights near the nest box. Unlike with other, smaller birds, you should never inspect or disturb the nest box. Clean it out thoroughly at the end of the brooding season.

The incubation period lasts about a month, and young owls will need to grow for about two months before they can fly on their own. Be aware that nestling owls are a noisy bunch. They may screech for food all night, and some homeowners find the noise keeps them awake.

TOOLS & MATERIALS

Tape measure

Carpenter's pencil

½" exterior-grade plywood

¾" exterior-grade plywood

½" wood dowel

Speed square

Circular saw

Power drill & bits

Jigsaw

Router or rotary tool

Waterproof wood glue

Mallet or hammer

1⅝" deck screws

1½ × 10½" scrap piece

1" deck screws

(1) 3" stainless steel butt hinge

1⅜" brass barrel bolt

Wood putty

Putty knife

Sandpaper

Paintbrush

Exterior gloss white paint

CUT LIST

(2) ¾ × 17½ × 20" front & back

(1) ½ × 15 × 22" roof panel long

(1) ½ × 15 × 21½" roof panel short

(1) ¾ × 10½ × 20" floor

(1) ¾ × 1½ × 10½" wall brace

(1) 1½ × 3½ × 7" mounting brace

(2) ½ × 4¾" front ledge dowel, long

(2) ½ × 3¾" front ledge dowel, medium

(2) ½ × 2¾" front ledge dowel, short

HOW TO BUILD A
BARN OWL A-FRAME

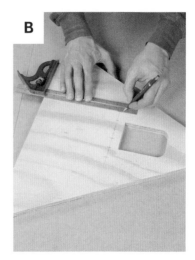

1 Cut all the pieces to the dimensions on the cut list. Bevel one end of each roof section and both short edges of the floor to 30°. Drill a grid of ½" drainage holes in the floor.

2 Measure, mark, and cut two equilateral triangles from the front and back pieces. The triangles should have 20" sides, 60° angles, and be 17⅜" high. Decide which side will be the bottom and measure up 8". Make a mark at this point, centered side to side [**fig. A**]. Use this as the center point for an arch-top doorway 3" wide by 4" tall. Drill an access hole and use a jigsaw to cut out the entrance. Sand the edges smooth.

3 Measure and mark a line of six ½" holes centered side to side ½" below the entrance and with ½" between each hole [**fig. B**]. Choose the rougher face to be the inside of the front, and rout or cut 8"-long kerfs, centered side to side, every ¾" up from the bottom of the front to the bottom of the entrance. (This will be a climbing ladder for the fledglings.)

4 Drill out the ledge dowel holes using a ½" bit. Coat the inside of each dowel hole with wood glue and tap the dowels in place (the two center dowels project 4" out; the next two on either side, 3"; and the outside dowels, 2" [**fig. C**].

5 Measure and mark for a 10" wide by 4" high cleanout door centered along the bottom of the front. Use the jigsaw to cut out the door. Drill a triangle of ½" vent holes at the point of the back (this will be the top).

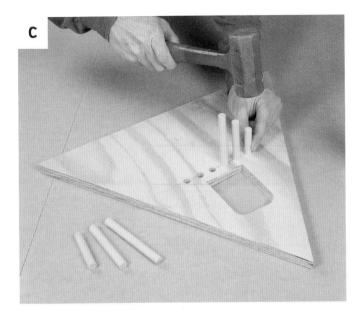

C

6 Drill pilot holes and glue and screw the front to the floor using 1⅝" deck screws. Ensure that the bottom is flush and the bevels on each end of the floor match the side angles of the front. Fasten the back on the opposite edge of the floor in the same way.

7 Screw a 1½"–wide by 10½"–long scrap as a brace between the front and the back, as close to the top as possible without blocking the back's ventilation holes. Position the shorter roof panel in place so that the overlap on front and back is exactly the same and the beveled edge is aligned with the top of the front and back (the bottom edge will project below the floor, so you need to work on bolsters). Position the longer roof panel overlapping the first so that its edge bevel aligns with the first panel's face. When you're sure that the panel is positioned correctly, drill pilot holes every few inches down into the front and back edges. Glue and screw the roof to the front and back with 1" deck screws [**fig. D**].

8 Fasten the opposite roof panel in the same manner. Position the door on the front and mark the front and door for the barrel bolt centered at the top and the butt hinge between the bottom and the floor. Remove the door; fasten the latch receiver to the top of the door and one hinge leaf to the bottom. Fasten the other hinge leaf to the bottom and the latch male to the front of the A-frame.

9 Putty over all the screw heads and sand smooth. Finish the A-frame, except for the ends of the ledge dowels, with a clear, no-VOC sealant. Paint the ends of the dowels gloss white. Decide where you'll mount the A-frame and level and screw the brace in place (it should be at least 12 to 15 feet above the ground). Slide the rear roof overhang over the brace so that the fit is snug and then screw the A-frame to the brace by driving 2" deck screws through the roof panels and into the ends of the brace.

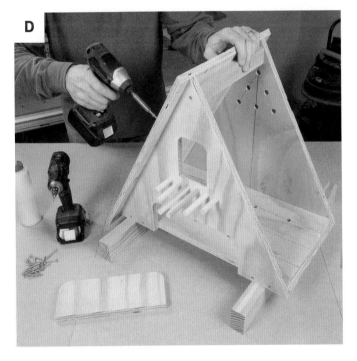

D

BARRED OWL NEST BOX

For such a large bird, the barred owl is incredibly agile in flight. It flies nearly silently and can actually hover before striking. This is something no rodent wants to see.

A simple, large box such as this is not only a perfect sanctuary for a secretive bird, it can also be an ideal blank canvas for your creative brainstorms. You could stencil black silhouettes on the body of the box to add a sense of drama or paint it in pastels for a splash of color where there might not normally be any. Really, it's just an outlet for your artistic intentions waiting to happen. The box itself may be most of the reward for providing a home for barred owls.

Owl lovers have to resign themselves to not enjoying many of the pleasures of birdwatching that can be enjoyed with other species. To start with, owls are—for the most part—nocturnal. That means you'll have to stay up late and be vigilant if you want to see one in action. Hosting barred owls is a more hands-off proposition than creating a nesting site for a smaller, more high-maintenance bird. This species, like almost all other owls, is a quiet hunter that largely takes care of itself. Few

predators stalk the barred owl or its offspring and eggs. But putting up a suitable nest box is a good way to offer a home to what can be a very useful predator itself.

You'll need to have a fairly heavily wooded property to accommodate a barred owl; the bird loves forests and prefers not to deal with the noise and chaos of human activity. But if your property fits the bill, you'll be providing lodging to a hunter who dines on many undesirables, from mice to snakes and lizards.

Barred owls can weigh more than two pounds and are just slightly smaller than a great horned owl. They also spend a long time in any nest site because the incubation and fledging period is much longer than it is for songbirds. All that means that this construction is meant to be as durable as it is handsome. Focus on measuring and marking the cuts correctly, make them with a steady hand, and the box will come together without much fuss.

TOOLS & MATERIALS

Tape measure

Straight edge

Carpenter's pencil

¾" exterior grade plywood

Circular saw

Power drill & bits

Jigsaw, router, or rotary tool

(2) 6" heavy-gauge T straps

Waterproof wood glue

2" deck screws

Silicone sealant

(4) #6 × ¾" (1.9 cm) stainless steel panhead screws

CUT LIST

(2) ¾ × 18 × 24" front & back

(2) ¾ × 16½ × 24" sides

(1) ¾ × 16½ × 16½" floor

(1) ¾ × 18 × 22" roof

HOW TO BUILD A
BARRED OWL NEST BOX

1 Cut all the pieces to the dimensions on the cut list. Drill five ¾" holes in the floor in an X pattern. Be sure that any hole is at least 1¼" in from the edge. Drill three holes spaced equidistance along one end of each side. The holes should be 2½" in from the edge.

2 Measure, mark, and cut the 10 × 10" entry hole centered along one end of the front (this will be the top of the front). Use a jigsaw to cut the opening [**fig. A**].

C

Cut a series of ⅛" –deep horizontal kerfs for a climbing ladder on the inside of the front. Make the kerfs starting 2" up from the bottom to right beneath the entrance.

3 Use the crossbar of a T strap to mark the location of the T strap and its mounting holes, at the top and bottom of the back. The T straps should be centered side to side.

4 Drill pilot holes and glue and screw one end of a side to an edge of the floor using 2" deck screws. Fasten the opposite side in the same way.

5 Position the front overlapping the sides and flush with the floor. Drill pilot holes and glue and screw the front to the sides and the floor using 2" deck screws [**fig. B**]. Fasten the back in the same way.

6 Lay a bead of silicone sealant all around the tops of the sides, front, and back [**fig. C**] and set the roof on top of the walls (it should be flush with the sides and back and overhanging the front). Drill pilot holes and then screw the roof to the body with 2" deck screws.

7 Screw the mounting T straps to the back with the #6 × ¾" stainless steel panhead screws [**fig. D**]. Mount the box 12 to 15 feet above the ground.

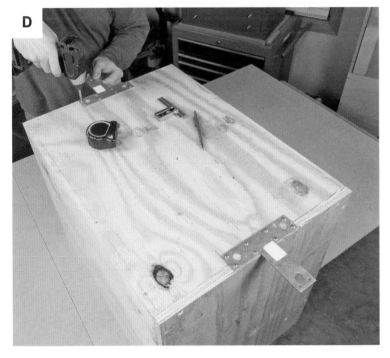

D

WOOD DUCK DORM

The male wood duck is one of the more stunning birds you're likely to attract to your yard — but you'll need plenty of space, and a body of water nearby.

Taking design cues from the flashy male of the couple for whom this lodging is intended, this is one very attention-grabbing structure. It features a black racing strip with a teal green roof and white body. The combination is striking and pleasingly unexpected in any wild setting. Even when the ducks aren't home, this structure will give your yard a wonderful visual.

The good news is that because available cavity sites are fewer and fewer, wood ducks will readily use an available nesting box—giving you plenty of opportunities to watch these beautiful and interesting birds in action. However, to actually attract ducks, you'll need the right surroundings. Start with the fact that wood ducks, like any duck, are water birds. That's why they normally nest on the borders of a marsh, in low wetlands, or along waterways. It's best if there is a significant body of water close to your property. If you have a sizable pond in your backyard, that may do the trick.

Ducks prefer low-lying vegetation, such as shrubs, in which to hide and forage. The birds eat a varied diet that can include acorns, blackberries, snails, millet, beetles, caterpillars, smartweed/knotweed, and much more. The more varied the landscape around your home and in the region at large, the better the chances that wood ducks will make a home there.

Although adult wood ducks have a limited number of predators (hunters are top of the list), the eggs are attractive to a number of thieves. That's why it's a wise move to add a predator hole guard to this or any wood duck nesting box.

However you outfit it, you can personalize the box by changing up the color scheme or even going with a much more traditional look by keeping the box natural. You can make the construction process a little simpler by doing without the strips of balsa wood on the front and roof, but, of course, you can also make the design more complex by adding layers with thinner strips of balsa wood.

TOOLS & MATERIALS

Tape measure
Carpenter's pencil
¼" exterior grade plywood
¾" exterior grade plywood
Circular or table saw
Miter saw
Power drill & bits
Router
Waterproof wood glue
French curve
Jigsaw
Sandpaper
¼ × 6 × 18" hardware cloth
Utility knife
Staple gun
Staples
2" deck screws
6d 2" galvanized casing nails
Speed square
Hammer
Brads
Wood putty
Putty knife
1" paintbrush
Painter's tape
Exterior gloss black paint
Exterior gloss white paint
Exterior gloss teal green paint
(2) 2" barrel bolts
Black iron pole or PVC painted black
Pipe straps

continued on page 126

HOW TO BUILD A
WOOD DUCK DORM

A

B

1 Cut all the pieces to the dimensions on the cut list. Cut the marked side panel into two pieces. Bevel one end of the front and back to 15°. Make a 15° cut across one end of each side. Drill ¼" drainage holes in an X pattern on the floor. Measure and mark a cut line on one side, 4" up from the end opposite the angled cut. Cut the marked side panel into two pieces.

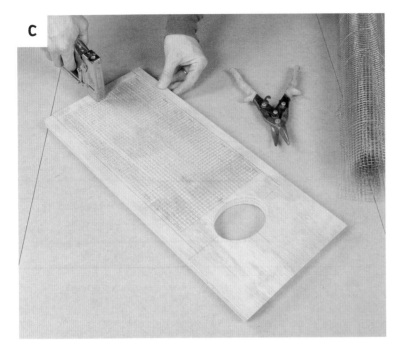

2 Rout or cut a finger notch in the 4" section of the cut side, centered side to side on one 8" edge. Glue the 23½"-long plywood strip to the shorter face of the front, centered side to side [**fig. A**]. Cut the top of the plywood strip to match the 15° bevel at the top of the front.

3 Secure the front face down. Measure and mark the center of the entry hole 19½" up from the bottom and centered side to side on the inside face. Draw crosshairs centered on the mark, with a 4" horizontal line and 3" vertical line. Trace an oval using a French curve between the ends of the crosshair marks [**fig. B**].

4 Drill an access hole and use a jigsaw to cut out the oval entry hole. Turn it over and use sandpaper to smooth any tear-out or roughness around the inside of the hole. Center the ¼" hardware cloth strip side to side on the inside face of the front, running from ¾" above the bottom to just below the entry hole. Staple it in place [**fig. C**].

5 Position one side against one edge of the floor, flush with the side and the bottom. Drill pilot holes and glue and screw the side to the floor with 2" deck screws.

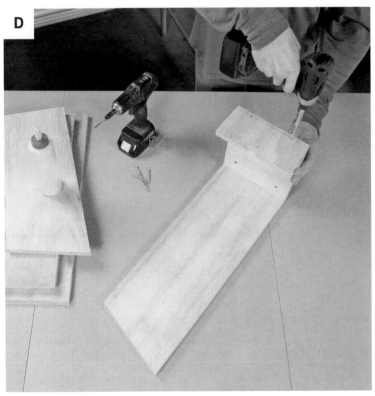

6 Position the 4" cut section in the same way on the opposite edge of the bottom (the finger notch should be at the top). Drill pilot holes and glue and screw the section to the bottom with 2" deck screws [**fig. D**].

continued from page 124

CUT LIST

(1) ¾ × 9½ × 23⅛" front
(1) ¾ × 9½ × 25½" back
(2) ¾ × 8 × 25" sides
(1) ¾ × 11 × 11" roof
(1) ¾ × 8 × 8" floor
(1) ¼ × 5 × 23½" front plywood stripe
(1) ¼ × 5 × 11" front plywood stripe

E

7 Align the back with the sides and bottom (the top of the back should sit ¼" above the top of the side to allow a vent strip at the top of the full side). Drill pilot holes and glue and screw the back to the sides and bottom. Repeat the process to attach the front.

8 Position the top of the cut side (the cleanout door) on top of the 4" section. It should fit snugly between the front of the back but still move enough to open. If necessary, sand or trim a small amount off one long edge until it moves freely between the front and back. Use a speed square to mark a vertical line 1" down from the top (angle cut) end of the section and then transfer that mark to the front and the back.

Note: The marks need to be positioned exactly horizontally across the side to ensure the door will swing open.

Drill small pilot holes and secure the section in place with brads that will act as hinges [**fig. E**].

F

9 Putty over all screw heads and sand smooth. Paint the front and roof strips first. They should be painted gloss black (protect the adjacent surfaces with painter's tape). Paint all exposed areas of the roof teal green and then paint the body of the birdhouse white.

10 Screw the barrel bolts on the bottom of the side to hold the cleanout door in place. Glue the short balsa wood strip to the roof, centered side to side. Position the roof across the front and back walls, centered in all directions. Drill pilot holes and glue and nail the roof to the front and back [**fig. F**]. Mount the house 10 feet [3 m] above the ground on a black iron pole or PVC pole that has been painted black. Attach the house with pipe straps spaced every 3" up the back.

One of the most distinctive-looking birds, woodpeckers are a brilliant and unmistakable presence in any wooded area. The pileated woodpecker shown here is one of the most common species.

When it comes to natural birdhouses, you can't do better than making one from the remains of a tree. This is perhaps the finest example of recycling materials into a nest box that will blend right in with the surroundings. Although it may not be as attention-grabbing and colorful as other projects in this book, this is one of the most comfortable and adaptable nest box designs for the intended occupant. Although this design was created for the relatively large woodpecker, you can use smaller logs to create more modest nest boxes to attract songbirds to a suburban home.

As designed, the birdhouse is meant to draw a pair of pileated woodpeckers, who prefer a wooded setting—especially one with dead or fallen trees. The birds will dig at dead wood in search of carpenter ants that are a mainstay in their diet. However, they are happy to eat other insects, including termites, grasshoppers, and beetle larvae, and will feast on wild fruit, such as blackberries and sumac berries. They will also gladly partake of a suet feeder if you put one up.

This birdhouse is meant to be stuffed full of wood shavings because the behavior of a woodpecker in search of a nest is to excavate the cavity before occupying it. The removable floor of this structure allows you to clean the birdhouse out after the brooding season, but you should refill it with wood shavings (which may entail stuffing them through the entry hole after you've replaced the floor because the house is meant to be permanently fixed to a large tree). It's a good idea to add a hole guard to ensure against predators getting at the large, delicious woodpecker eggs.

The birdhouse's design is simple but requires a good deal of elbow grease to complete, unless you happen to have access to a bandsaw. Although you could paint the roof, there really is no point; the structure is meant to look entirely natural within its surroundings, so decoration works against the main purpose.

HOW TO BUILD A
WOODPECKER LOG HOME

TOOLS & MATERIALS

Tape measure

Carpenter's pencil

¾" plywood

26"–long × 14"–dia. log (Actual dimensions don't have to match exactly; slightly larger is better.)

Bandsaw or handsaw

Miter saw

C-clamps or bar clamps

Power drill & bits

4" deck screws

4" hole saw

Wood shavings

3" flathead structural screws

Hammer

6d galvanized penny nails

CUT LIST

(1) ¾ × 14 × 16" roof

(1) ¾ × 12 × 24" back

A

B

1 Cut the roof and back to the dimensions on the cut list. Bevel one edge of the back to 20°, and bevel one long edge of the roof to 20°. Cut an even, roughly 2", slice off the log, end to end. You can use a bandsaw for this if you have one available; otherwise, use a handsaw [**fig. A**].

2 Cut one end of the log to a 20° angle so that the longer edge is to the cut side of the log [**fig. B**]. Slice off the remaining three sides of the log as you did the back.

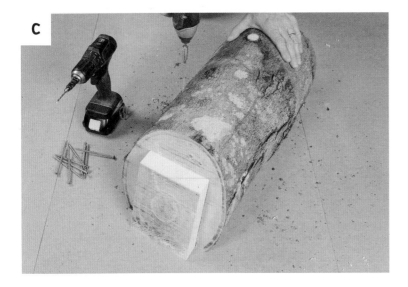

3 Reconstruct these three sides around the squared-off core. Drill pilot holes and screw each side to the front along the long edges. Remove the core. Fasten the back by drilling pilot holes and screwing the back to the two sides (make sure the beveled end is flush with the top angle cut) [**fig. C**].

4 Cut a 1½" slice off the end of the core for the floor. Sit the log house on its back and use a 4" hole saw to drill the entry hole centered 16" up from the bottom.

5 Drill pilot holes and screw the roof to the sides, with the beveled edge flush to the back and the roof centered side to side [**fig. D**].

6 Sit the log on top of the floor. Pack the inside of the house with wood shavings and then secure the floor in place with 3" flathead structural screws [**fig. E**]. Choose a location carefully because the house will be immovable once you've attached it to the tree. Toenail it through the roof and sides to the tree, about 20 feet above the ground, using 6d galvanized penny nails.

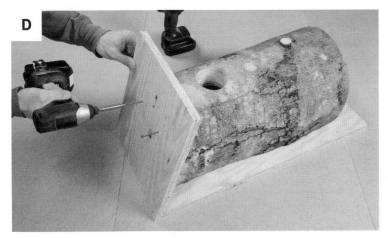

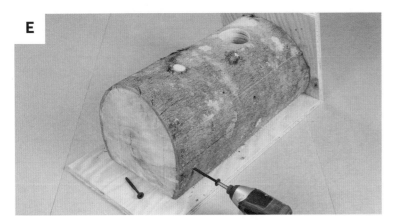

FABULOUS FEEDER PROJECTS

EVERYONE LOVES A FREE MEAL, and birds are no different. Although a few species will only turn to feeders in the event that they can't find a food source — such as in the winter — most birds are instantly attracted to a yard with a feeder in it. As long as the feeder is kept filled with food.

As pragmatic as these structures are, they can still be an opportunity to exercise your creativity and craft a decorative feature for the yard. Feeders are, in fact, often more visible and center stage than the birdhouses themselves. They are also a chance to watch a variety of birds in action because, unlike a birdhouse, feeders can attract multiple species to congregate more or less peacefully.

Of course, every bird has its own preferences when it comes to food. That means you'll need to have some idea of the birds native to your area before you spend time and effort putting up a feeder and money buying a seed mix.

Regardless of the feeder, certain rules apply. Always keep the feeder stocked with food or birds will ignore it as an unreliable source of nutrition. Keeping feeders clean is also important, to avoid spreading disease among bird populations. Keep an eye out for any moldy or rotting food and remove it at once. Remember, bird health is the most important aspect of inviting feathered visitors into your backyard.

Gravity bird feeders ensure a minimum of maintenance in keeping the feeder stocked because you can put a great deal of food in the feed tube. This can be essential: if a feeder runs out of food, birds may get the message that it's not a reliable source of nutrition and won't return. Of course, the best gravity feeder of all is the one that looks sharp while feeding your feathered friends. And you'll be hard pressed to find one that is quite as distinctive and fun as this fairly accurate re-creation of the nearly defunct but once-ubiquitous phone booth.

Most of the details are represented, except for the actual phone—in its place, you'll be filling the booth with the bird seed mix of your choice. You'll be able to see the level of remaining bird seed thanks to realistic windows cut from thick plastic sheets, the type of material used to create windows for architectural models.

On the subject of models, much of the work that goes into this project is fine-detail crafting that requires accurate measurements and a steady hand. It's as much an exercise in model-making as it is in woodworking, but the results speak for themselves. Not only will the birds have an ample feeder that allows several songbirds to perch and eat at once, you'll also have a yard decoration second to none that is sure to be an amusing conversation piece at your next cookout.

So, yes, you could buy a bland gravity feeder at retail, one that would cost you a pretty penny and be little style and mostly function. Or, you could save some money, spend some fun time in the workshop, and craft your own unique design full of whimsy and the look of yesteryear, one that the birds will enjoy every bit as much as the humans in your yard. It's your call!

TOOLS & MATERIALS

Tape measure

Carpenter's pencil

¼" balsa wood sheet

¾" exterior grade plywood

Circular saw

Waterproof wood glue

Wood putty

Sandpaper

Power drill & bits

¾" × ¾" square dowel (cut from hardwood)

Small C-clamps

2" exterior trim screws

Masking or painter's tape

Exterior silver spray paint

Paintbrush

Black oil-based model paint

Red oil-based model paint

6 mil acetate

Metal straight edge

Utility knife (with new blade) or coping saw

Silicone adhesive or two-part epoxy

¼ × 6" toggle eyebolt

1¾" neoprene fender washer

CUT LIST

(2) ¼ × 4½ × 4½" roof cores

(1) ¼ × 5½ × 5½" roof trim

(4) ¾ × ¾ × 10" corner posts

(4) ¼ × ⅝ × 3" headers

(6) ¼ × ⅝ × 3" side & back braces

(4) ¼ × 1 × 10¼" inch side posts

(4) ¼ × ¾ × 10¼" front & back posts

(3) ¼ × 1½ × 3" bottom panels

(1) ¼ × ½ × 8½" door divider

(2) ¼ × ½ × 1¼" door rails

(1) ¼ × ⅝ × 3" door bottom rail

(4) ¹⁄₃₂ × 4⅜ × 9⅝" windows

(1) ¾ × 11 × 11" tray bottom

(2) ¾ × 1½ × 11" tray sides

(2) ¾ × 1½ × 12½" tray front & back

HOW TO BUILD A
PHONE BOOTH GRAVITY FEEDER

A

B

1 Cut the two roof cores and one roof ledge to size. Glue the roof cores to the roof ledge with the roof ledge overhanging the cores by ½" all around. Once the glue dries, drill a 1¼" access hole through the middle of the roof assembly for filling the feeder.

2 Cut the four posts to ¾ × ¾ × 10". Glue the posts to the inside roof core so they're even with its corners. Wait until the glue dries and then reinforce these joints with 2" exterior screws driven down through the roof and into the posts **[fig. A]**.

3 Putty over the screw heads and sand as desired. Mask off the inside roof core and posts. Paint the outside surfaces of the roof silver. Keep paint off of the inside and the post surfaces to ensure adhesive will stick better to these areas.

4 Cut the tray base to shape and mark the post locations on it. Center the posts on the tray. Attach the tray base to the posts with 2" screws driven up through the bottom.

5 Cut the headers, braces, bottom panels, and posts according to the dimensions on the cut list. You'll use these to assemble three frames for the sides and back of the feeder.

Note: The posts for the sides are wider than the posts for the back in order to overlap them at the phone booth corners.

6 Mark the posts for the header, brace, and bottom panel locations. Glue the frames together with waterproof wood glue. Apply narrow tape across the glue joints to hold them closed until the glue cures.

7 Cut a header, door divider, door rails, bottom rail, and posts to create a door trim framework. Mark the posts and header for the door divider, door rails, and bottom rail locations. Glue these pieces together with waterproof wood glue [**fig. B**].

8 Paint the outside faces and edges of the four frames. Paint the headers black, the bottom panels red, and the other parts silver.

9 Cut four window panels from acetate using a craft or utility knife guided by a straightedge. Two or three scoring cuts will easily cut cleanly through the plastic [**fig. C**]. Attach the windows to the posts with thin beads of silicone adhesive or two-part epoxy. Press the windows against the posts all along the glue joints to spread the adhesive, which will improve its bonding strength.

10 Glue the four trim frames to the windows with thin beads of silicone adhesive or two-part epoxy. Apply strips of masking or painter's tape over the corners of the phone booth to hold the trim frameworks in position until the adhesive cures [**fig. D**].

11 Cut the pieces for the tray's front, back, and sides according to the dimensions listed. Fasten them around the perimeter of the tray base with glue and 2" exterior screws [**fig. E**]. Install the toggle eyebolt and neoprene washer into the feeder top. Hang the feeder in your preferred location.

This wonderfully evocative birdfeeder brings to mind the lazy days of deep summer and the pace of a country home. The design mimics a full-size porch swing, and the simple lines are pleasing to the eye—as are the birds that will flock to the easily accessible banquet.

This is the most basic type of feeder—a simple tray with a screen bottom so that the feeder itself doesn't get gunked up and the feed won't get moldy. The occasional summer shower will just drip right through. The screen also ensures that only small bits of husks and seeds make their way through to the ground below, meaning that any mess should be modest (that's also the reason for the thick lip around the tray of the feeder). This design is sized to accommodate more than one bird, and several different species can use it comfortably without getting in each other's way.

Although you can always customize a design such as this, the nature of a porch swing look begs for the natural finish specified in this project. You can certainly paint it if you're looking for something a little more apparent among the greenery in your yard, but it's probably wisest to stick with white, so that you maintain the clean look of straight lines and simple structure.

TOOLS & MATERIALS

Tape measure

Carpenter's pencil

Fine wood file

¾" exterior grade plywood

½" exterior grade plywood

Miter or circular saw

Fiberglass window screen

Shears

Jigsaw or coping saw

Power drill & bits

2" deck screws

Staple gun (or hammer & landscaping staples)

Staples

Hammer

Finish nails

Paintbrush

Waterproof clear protecting finish

Metal straight edge

(4) 1" screw eyes

4' #16 jack chain

1" S hooks

#6 × 1¼" cabinet screws

CUT LIST

(1) ¾ × 1½ × 10" frame front

(1) ¾ × 1½ × 8½" frame back

(2) ¾ × 1½ × 7¾" frame sides

(2) ¾ × 2 × 7½" seat back posts

(4) ½ × 1 × 3" arm supports

(2) ½ × 1¼ × 9½" arms

(5) ½ × ¾ × 10" seat back slats

(1) 8 × 10" base screen

HOW TO BUILD A
PORCH SWING BIN FEEDER

1 Cut all the pieces to the dimensions on the cut list. Use shears to cut an 8 × 11" section of window screen. Cut one end of each frame side and one end of each seatback post to a 15° angle. Mark the arm pattern on the top of each arm and cut the arms to shape with a jigsaw or coping saw (see diagram opposite page). Round them into shape with a file, as necessary [**fig. A**].

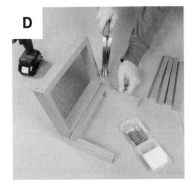

D

E

F

the posts so that they are spaced evenly up to the last slat, which should be flush with the top of the posts. Make key marks for each and then drill pilot holes and nail the rails to the posts with finish nails [**fig. D**].

6 Place an arm support at the front corner of the frame, perpendicular and flush to the front and bottom. Drill pilot holes and screw the post to the frame with 2" deck screws. Measure and mark 4" back from the front and fasten another support with its front edge at the mark, as you did the first. Repeat for the opposite side.

7 Position an arm across the supports on one side, with the straight edge along the frame side and the front edge aligned with the front of the frame. Drill pilot holes and nail the arm to the supports and to the seatback post [**fig. E**]. Repeat with the opposite arm.

8 Finish all the surfaces of the feeder except for the inside of the seat tray using a nontoxic, clear protecting finish. Attach screw eyes into the front of each arm, down into the front arm support, and into the top of the outer seatback posts on both sides [**fig. F**].

9 Attach four lengths of chain, one from each screw eye, and join them with an S hook. Hang the feeder by a chain suspended from a branch or overhang and connected to the S hook. Fill the feeder with your preferred seed mix.

2 Join the frame front and the straight end of one frame side by drilling a pilot hole and screwing the pieces together with a 2" deck screw [**fig. B**]. Attach the second frame side to the opposite end of the front in the same manner.

Note: Ensure the frame side angle cuts are oriented in the same direction.

3 Complete the base frame by screwing the frame back between the back angle cuts of the frame sides. Align the outside face of the back with the shortest point of the angle cuts. Drill pilot holes and screw the sides to the back. Staple the screen panel onto the bottom edges, flush with the outside of the frame [**fig. C**].

4 Drill pilot holes and screw the first seatback post to the frame side, with the angled end of the post flush with the bottom of the frame. Use 2" deck screws and repeat with the opposite seatback post. Measure and mark the center point between the two along the frame back.

5 Lay the structure on its back. Position the seatback slats across

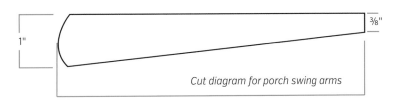

Cut diagram for porch swing arms

3/8"

1"

This interesting novelty design relies on an inside joke: creating a bird feeder based on the traditional farm dummy used to scare birds away from fields of crops. Fortunately, songbirds aren't spooked by a scarecrow and find a suet feeder irresistible anyway.

Suet feeders are a popular option with a great number of birds, including aggressive species, such as starlings and red wing blackbirds. Using a cage feeder such as the one in this project limits accessibility for larger, more aggressive birds. Of course, suet cakes are some of the most delicious food for birds, and that fact isn't lost on mice, squirrels, and raccoons. That's why this feeder hangs from a thin chain that makes it difficult for any furry pest to get to the food.

Do be aware that the feeder should be positioned out of direct sun. Suet feed has a high degree of fat in it and can spoil rapidly when exposed to high heat or long periods of direct sunlight.

Although you shouldn't get any finish on the inside of the cage "body," you can go wild otherwise. You can paint the arms and body the color of a denim shirt and the pants a nice khaki green. If you're handy with a jigsaw or coping saw, cut a floppy hat when you cut the circle for the head or add other details, such as fingers or shoes.

TOOLS & MATERIALS

Tape measure

Carpenter's pencil

1 × 6 × 6' cedar board

Circular or table saw

Sandpaper

Waterproof wood glue

Power drill & bits

2" deck screws

1½" deck screws

Wire mesh suet feeder

Fender washers

Loose straw or crafting raffia

Silicone sealant

Floral wire

Twine

Putty knife

Wood putty

[2] 1" stainless steel screw eyes

#16 jack chain

Suet brick

CUT LIST

[1] ¾ × 4" dia. head

[1] ¾ × 3 × 8½" top

[2] ¾ × 2 × 6¾" sides

[1] ¾ × 2 × 5½" bottom

[2] ¾ × 2 × 8" arms

[2] ¾ × 1⅛ × 8⅛" legs

HOW TO BUILD A
SCARECROW SUET FEEDER

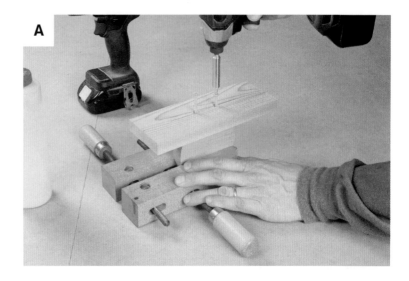

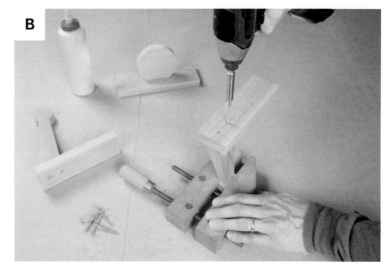

1 Cut all the pieces to the dimensions on the cut list. Cut the arms according to the pattern (see diagram opposite page). Sand the curved edges of the arms and head smooth. Clip an edge of the head to create a flat surface for attaching the head to the shoulders.

2 Measure and mark the center of the roof. Glue and screw the head to this point, driving two 2" deck screws from the opposite side of the roof [**fig. A**]. Drill pilot holes and glue and screw each arm to one end of each side.

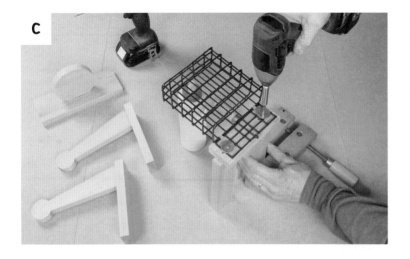

C

3 Position one leg ¼" in from one side of the bottom and centered back to front. Glue and screw it in place. Repeat with the second leg.

4 Screw the feeder cage access door to the leg assembly using 2" deck screws and fender washers [**fig. C**].

5 Drill pilot holes and glue and screw the sides to the floor.

6 Drill pilot holes and glue and screw the head assembly centered on top of the sides. Glue down a skirt of raffia or straw around the base of the head using a heavy layer of silicone sealant. Wire long cuffs of straw around the end of each arm using floral wire. Apply silicone sealant around the cuffs and wrap them in twine to hide the wire [**fig. D**].

7 Putty over exposed screw heads and sand the dried putty smooth. Finish with a clear exterior wood sealant. Drill a starter hole and attach a screw eye into each end of the roof (the shoulders of the scarecrow). Place a suet brick into the feeder body and hang the feeder with chain or cable from a tree branch or sturdy overhang in an area with a clear line of sight all around.

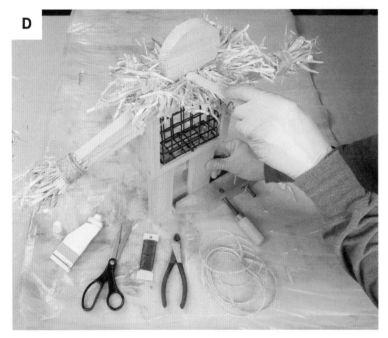

D

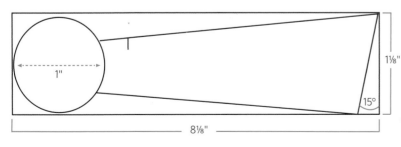

1"

1⅛"

15°

8⅛"

Cut diagram for scarecrow arms

lthough you can find flashier or more colorful designs for feeders, you won't find a better one that keeps your precious birdfeed safe from furry food thieves. This construction is based on a pivoting design that uses moving rungs and a sliding feed bin gate to deny a squirrel or raccoon access to the food. Coincidentally, the feeder can provide some unexpected hilarity. Frustrated squirrels try to figure out just what the heck is going on as the platform tilts under their weight and keeps them away from what seemed like such an easy meal.

This feeder requires a fair amount of work and demands that you devote attention to detail. But the end result is a great deterrence to common yard pests that can empty a bird feeder in a couple of trips and keep beautiful songbirds from calling your yard home. You'll find that the feeder attracts several different species of small birds and will be difficult for larger birds, such as crows or jays, to use—an added benefit when it comes to providing for smaller, more vulnerable songbirds.

Of course, as involved as the design is, you can always put your own signature on it. Paint the rungs different colors for an interesting look or paint the entire structure if you like—there are enough parts to make a real color statement. You can also stain the wood light or dark or even use a more exotic wood if you prefer.

In any case, the feeder must be post- or pole-mounted to work correctly. You can use a 4 × 4" fence post with the flange mounting system described in the steps below, or you can use cast iron or PVC pipe with a mated flange to mount the feeder. In any case, paint or disguise the pole to blend into the yard and complement the look of the feeder.

TOOLS & MATERIALS

Tape measure

Carpenter's pencil

1 × 8" cedar board

2 × 2" cedar board

½" wood dowels

Miter or table saw

Sandpaper

Power drill & bits, or drill press

Drill bit depth gauge

Waterproof wood glue

2" deck screws

Staple gun

Staples

Hook-and-eye latch

(2) 1½" stainless steel hinges

1½" deck screws

¾" fender washers

CUT LIST

(1) ¾ × 5½ × 7¼" front

(1) ¾ × 5½ × 8⅛" back

(2) ¾ × 6½ × 10⅜" sides

(1) ¾ × 4⅞ × 9" roof, front

(1) ¾ × 5⅞ × 9" roof, back

(1) ¾ × 1¾ × 5½" front lip

(1) ¾ × 5 × 5½" floor

(1) ¾ × 3 × 5½" floor pivot brace

(2) ¾ × 1¾ × 20" base sides

(2) ¾ × 1¾ × 7½" base ends

(1) ¾ × 5 × 9" counterweight

(4) ½"–dia. × 8½" rungs

(2) ½"–dia. × 3" feeder pivot dowels

(1) 1½ × 1½ × 9" stop block

(2) ¾ × 1½ × 4¾" pivot arms

(2) ¾ × 1 × 3½" long post flange

(2) ¾ × 1 × 5½" short post flange

(1) ¾ × 8" aluminum bar

(1) 5 × 6" landscape fabric chute

(1) ¾ × 8" aluminum bar

(2) ¾ × 4¼ × 7¾" chute triangle brace

(1) ¾ × 5½ × 7¾" chute

(1) ¾ × 1 × 9" base stop

HOW TO BUILD A
SQUIRREL-PROOF FEEDER

A

B

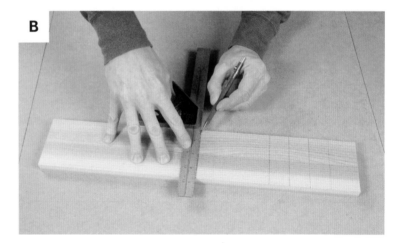

1 Cut all the pieces to the dimensions on the cut list. Cut the outline of the feeder sides to match the template on page 157 [**fig. A**]. Be very careful when cutting the 90° roof angle; the point of the roof is inset from the center on the side walls because the front of the feeder has a foot that accommodates the feed bin. [Mark the cuts clearly first and then check them against the diagram to ensure that they are precisely accurate.]

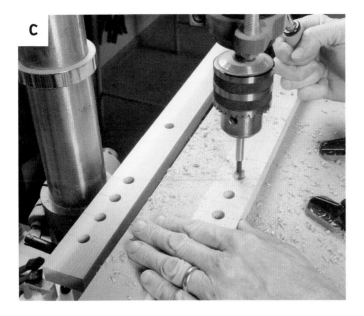

C

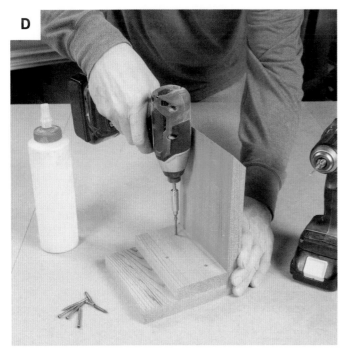

D

2 Bevel one long edge of the front and back roof panels to 45°. Bevel one short edge of the front and back walls to 45°. Bevel one short edge of the chute to 60°. Round off the ends of the pivot arms with sandpaper or a sander and drill ³⁄₁₆" holes in each end of each arm ¾" in from the end and centered side to side.

3 Mark the holes for both base sides at the same time. Starting from one end, mark the placement of the first dowel rung 1¾" in from an end (all the marks should be centered edge to edge). Make a second mark 1¼" from the first and two more, each 1¼" in from the preceding mark. Mark the feeder body pivot locations exactly 10" in from the end [**fig. B**].

4 Use a depth gauge on a ½" drill bit to drill ½"-deep holes at each of the marks on the base sides [**fig. C**]. Clean the holes up as necessary with sandpaper and check that the end of a ½" dowel fits in each hole and can turn freely.

5 Drill pilot holes and glue and screw the back to one side of the floor with 2" screws; the back's beveled edge should be at the top, and the bottom should be flush with the floor sides and bottom. Glue and screw the floor pivot brace to the floor, running side to side [**fig. D**].

6 Drill pilot holes and glue and screw a side wall to the floor, flush to the floor and back, using 2" deck screws. Screw the chute to the two triangle braces, along the longest edge of the braces. The braces should be centered along the chute side to side, with about 3" between them (the chute's beveled edge should be flush with the high side edge of the brace). Screw the chute in place on the floor, low side facing front, driving screws up underneath into the center of the braces.

7 Screw the first side to the edge of the chute. Attach the opposite side wall to the opposite side of the floor in the same fashion, so that it mirrors the first side wall. Screw it to the opposite edge of the chute.

E

F

G

8 Drill pilot holes and glue and screw the lip to the floor, between the two side cutouts, using 2" deck screws. Drill pilot holes and screw the sides to the lip. Drill pilot holes and screw the sides to the front using 2" deck screws; the front's beveled edge should be flush with the top angle cuts of the sides.

9 Measure and mark the locations of the feeder pivot dowels 3" in from the back on both sides of the feeder body and ⅞" up from the bottom. Use a depth gauge to drill the pivot holes 2¼" deep at the marks. Check that the dowels fit and turn smoothly in the holes and adjust as necessary [**fig. E**].

10 With the construction still lying on its side, measure and mark the center point on the floor and draw a 3½" square around the center point. Glue and screw the short post flanges along opposite sides of the square using 1½" deck screws. Drill pilot

holes and glue and screw the long post flanges along the other edges, overlapping the short flanges.

11 Position the front roof panel so that the beveled edge is at the front, the top edge is flush with the point of the roof, and the panel overhangs equal amounts on both sides. Drill pilot holes and glue and screw the front roof panel in place.

12 Position the back roof panel overlapping the front panel at the peak. Make sure the panel is positioned correctly, with the side overhangs matching the front roof panel, and mark the location of the hinges on both roof panels. Mark the location of the latch on the rear overhang and the back. Remove the back roof panel and install the hinges and the hook for the fastener. Replace it and screw the hinge to the front roof and the catch for the hook on the back [**fig. F**].

13 Drill pilot holes and glue and screw one base side to an end with 2" deck screws. Screw the side to the opposite base end in the same way.

14 Set the partially assembled side outside-face down on a flat, level work surface. Slip all the rungs and the feeder body dowels into their respective holes. Slide the feeder body onto the pivot dowel with the front facing the rungs [**fig. G**]. Put the second pivot dowel in the opposite hole of the feeder body and slip the second base side onto the ends of the rungs and feeder body pivot dowel. Finally, drill pilot holes and screw the second base side to the ends with 2" exterior trim head screws.

15 Sit the feeder upright. Measure and mark the center point of the front roof panel edge and the front of the feeder (on the lip). Drill pilot holes and screw the aluminum bar to the roof ledge and lip [**fig. H**].

16 Slip the stop block into the space between the front of the feeder and the block guide. Place a pivot arm against the base side (it should be positioned so that the screw hole is halfway between the bottom and top of the side and so that it is almost directly parallel to the front of the feeder). Drill a pilot hole. Screw the end of the pivot arm to the base side, putting a ¾" fender washer between the arm and the base side and one on the outside between the screw head and the pivot. Leave the screw a little loose [**fig. I**]. Repeat with the opposite pivot arm.

17 Drill a pilot hole through the top end of one pivot arm into the stop block side and then screw the pivot arm to the stop block loosely, with a fender washer on the inside and outside [**fig. J**]. Repeat with the opposite arm and snug down all screws so that the pivot arms can move to accommodate the up-and-down motion of the stop block.

18 Drill pilot holes and glue and screw the counterweight in place on the end of the base opposite the rungs. Screw the feeder to the post through the flanges. Screw a ¾ × 1 × 9" piece behind the rear post flange to stop the base at 90° to the feeder when it's reset after a squirrel trips it. Fill the bin with a seed mix and test the force needed to move the rung side of the base down. If it is too sensitive, add a second counterweight board to the opposite side.

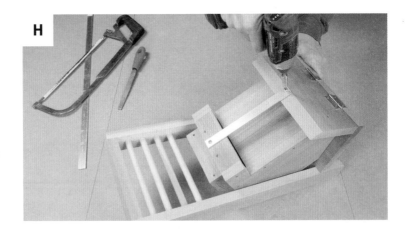

H

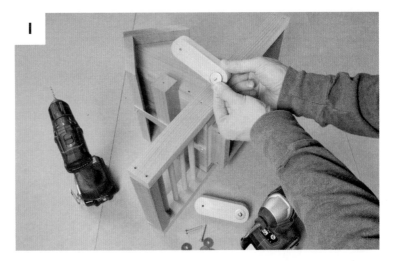

I

J

Want to add a splash of Japanese style to your backyard? How about a little flash of color with sophisticated architectural flair? Look no further. This basic tray feeder would be right at home in a Japanese tea garden and will provide an elegant addition to your landscape, as well as plenty of food to any hungry songsters that visit.

In keeping with a traditional Zen aesthetic, this feeder is all angles and subtle decorative elements. The construction requires some angle cuts and a couple of bevels that are easily achieved on a miter saw, but the result is rather stunning.

The feeder is meant to be hung, making it less accessible to hungry food thieves, such as squirrels and raccoons. The screened bottom allows air and moisture to flow through, preventing mold and mess inside the feeder tray. Just the same, keep in mind that birds are messy eaters, especially at tray feeders; the ground underneath will quickly be littered with smaller, seed-mix fillers and husks. That's why it's a good idea to hang the feeder over lush ornamental grass or, better yet, a bed of groundcover.

The red-and-black color scheme of this design adds a bit of drama to an otherwise understated, elegant look. But, of course, you can choose colors that are more to your taste. Given the small surface area the colors cover, you can actually go a bit wild in your choice of hues without risking much.

Regardless of what it looks like, the first and sacred rule of tray feeders is to keep them stocked. Unlike gravity or suet feeders, the seed mix will be consumed rather quickly in a bird-busy yard. If the feeder stands empty for a full day or several days, birds will figure out that it is not a reliable source of sustenance, and they will look to other yards for their meals.

TOOLS & MATERIALS

Tape measure

Carpenter's pencil

Jigsaw

1 × 6" cedar board

¼" balsa wood square dowel

Circular or table saw

Coarse metal screen or expanded metal sheet

Angle grinder or heavy-duty metal shears

Fiberglass window screen

Scissors or utility knife

Miter saw (optional)

Power drill & bits

Stapler

Staples

(4) 1" washer-head screws

2" deck screws

Waterproof wood glue

1½" stainless steel wood screws

Putty knife

Wood putty

Sandpaper

Paintbrush

Painter's tape

Exterior gloss black paint

Red oil-based model paint

Fender washers

Low- or no-VOC clear poly or light combination stain-poly finish

1" stainless steel screw eye

Silicone sealant

#16 chain

Bar clamps

CUT LIST

(2) ¾ × 4 × 9¾" posts

(2) ¾ × 8 × 10" roof panels

(2) ¾ × 1 × 10" tray sides

(2) ¾ × 1 × 6½" tray ends

(2) ¾ × 3 × 6" triangle gables

(1) ¾ × 2 × 4" brace

(4) ¼ × ¼ × 11" decorative roof rails

HOW TO BUILD A
ZEN TRAY FEEDER

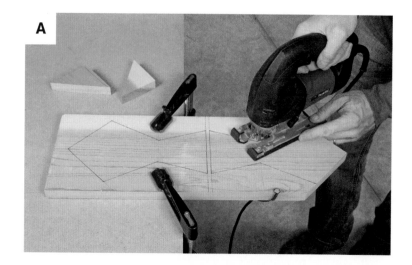

1 Cut all the parts to the dimensions on the cut list. Use a jigsaw to cut the blanks into posts (diagram, see page 157) and gables (diagram, see page 157) [**fig. A**].

2 Use an angle grinder or metal shears to cut an 8 × 10" section of metal screen or expanded metal sheet. Cut a rectangle of the window screen to the same dimensions. Bevel one long edge of each roof panel to 45°.

3 Build the birdseed tray by drilling pilot holes and gluing and screwing an 8" tray side overlapping the end of one tray end. Fasten the second tray end to the opposite end of the tray side in the same manner. Screw the opposite tray side to the tray ends in the same way to complete the tray frame.

4 Staple the window screen to the edges of the tray frame. Drill pilot holes and screw the metal screen over the landscape fabric and to the lip of the tray using 1" screws with finishing washers [**fig. B**].

5 Drill pilot holes and screw the brace between the two posts using 2" deck screws. The brace ends should be positioned vertically about 1" down from the top point of each post [**fig. C**].

6 Drill pilot holes and glue and screw the two roof panels together along their mitered edges. Mask off the roof subassembly for the decorative roof

rails and the gable diamonds and then paint the roof. Place the roof on top of the two roof posts so that the overhang on each end is equal and drill pilot holes and screw the roof to the posts with 1½" stainless steel wood screws [**fig. D**].

7 Position a gable in place at the underside of one roof end, inset about ¼" from the edge. Drill pilot holes and glue and screw the gable in place. Repeat at the opposite end of the roof with the second gable.

8 Putty over the screw holes in the roof and sand smooth. Touch up the roof. Use painter's tape to mask off the adjacent surfaces and paint the gables red. When the paint has dried, mask off a diamond in the center of each gable and paint it black. Paint the decorative roof rails gloss red.

9 Position the tray centered across the bottoms of the posts, with equal amounts on each side and each end.

Drill pilot holes through the expanded metal sheet and window screen into the bottoms of the posts and secure the tray to the posts with 1" washer-head screws [**fig. E**].

10 Finish the outside of the tray in a natural, no- or low-VOC protective finish. Carefully measure and make key marks for the placement of the decorative rails on each side of the roof [they are positioned about 1" in from each roof edge]. Sand one face of each rail and glue them, rough-face down, to the roof.

11 Attach a 1" stainless steel screw eye into the center of the roof crest and lay a bead of silicone sealant around the base of the screw eye. Use #16 chain to hang the feeder from an overhang or tree branch with a clear line of sight all around. Fill the tray with a seed mix.

TEMPLATES

CLASSIC BLUEBIRD HOUSE *page 30*

Cutting diagram for Classic Bluebird House

Roof	Front	Back	Floor	Side	Side
8½"	10"	14½"	4"	10¾	9¾

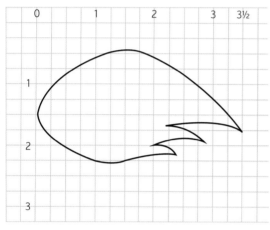

Wing diagram for Classic Bluebird House

THE BAT CAVE *page 36*

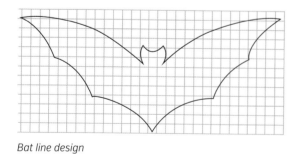

Bat line design

SPARROW MILK CARTON *page 98*

Cutting diagram for Sparrow Milk Carton

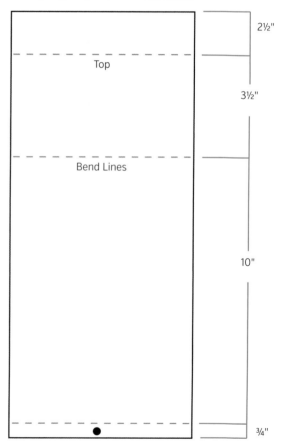

Top

Bend Lines

2½"

3½"

10"

¾"

MOURNING DOVE MONSTER LEDGE *page 106*

Cutting diagram for decorative elements

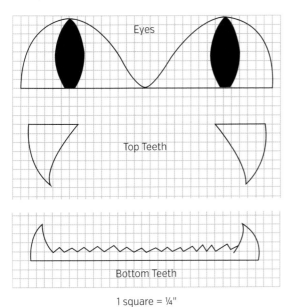

1 square = ¼"

ZEN TRAY FEEDER *page 154*

Cutting diagram for post

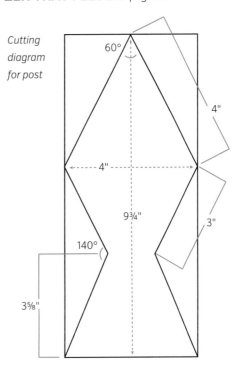

SQUIRREL-PROOF FEEDER *page 148*

Sideview of cutting diagram

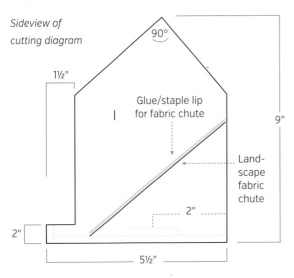

Cutting diagram for gable

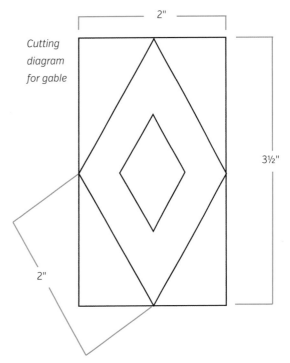

RESOURCES

American Bird Conservancy
888-247-3624
abcbirds.org

American Birding Association
800-850-2473
aba.org

American Ornithological Society
americanornithology.org

Bat Conservation International
800-538-BATS (2287)
batcon.org

BirdLife International
birdlife.org

BirdWatching
877-252-8141
birdwatchingdaily.com

Bird Watcher's Digest
800-879-2473
birdwatchersdigest.com

Birds & Blooms
birdsandblooms.com

Hawk Mountain Sanctuary
610-756-6961
hawkmountain.org

National Audubon Society
844-428-3826
audubon.org

North American Bluebird Society
513-300-8714
nabluebirdsociety.org

Purple Martin Conservation Association
814-833-7656
purplemartin.org

Raptor Research Foundation
raptorresearchfoundation.org

The Nature Conservancy
800-628-6860
nature.org

The National Wildlife Federation
800-822-9919
nwf.org

The Peregrine Fund: American Kestrel Partnership
208-362-3716
peregrinefund.org/projects/american-kestrel

Wild Birds Unlimited Nature Shop
317-571-7100
wildbirds.com or wbu.com

PHOTO CREDITS

INDEX